A Fabulous First Year and Beyond:

A Practical Guide for Pre-K
and Kindergarten Teachers

A Fabulous First Year and Beyond:
A Practical Guide for Pre-K and Kindergarten Teachers
By Vanessa J. Levin

Published by Teacherpreneur Press

ISBN: 0615630510
ISBN-13: 9780615630519

First Edition

With thanks, I dedicate this to:
Barbara Vissers, Norma Moon, and Nancy Pruett who supported and inspired me throughout my first year of teaching. Also to my colleague Olga Quintero who is a "teacher extraordinaire", role model, mentor, and friend.

CONTENTS

FORWARD

I am neuroscientist. I research the human brain. More specifically, I study how we feel what we feel, what makes us do what we do, and how that affects our mind, body and spirit. In my opinion, my profession is not nearly as impressive or as important as yours.

Like most human enterprises, education is a journey not a destination. Your student's journey begins with you. It is a journey that will affect all aspects of their lives, from the quality of their relationships, to their careers, to their personal happiness to their physical health.

Your job as a Pre-K or Kindergarten teacher is so very important because the experiences your students have in your classroom will determine whether or not they consider learning to be a positive or negative experience for years to come. The more positive you make this experience; the more likely they will be to develop positive attitudes about learning experiences and school in general. This is crucial because most experiences in life involve learning.

If you are successful, as your students go through life their brains will expect learning experiences to be positive, thereby anticipating and responding to them accordingly. A student who has developed a positive outlook about school may decide to continue his or her education instead of dropping out of high-school. Conversely, those students who have not had positive experiences may be impacted negatively and for the rest of their lives and for future generations to come.

Time and children are the most precious human resources. As a doctor, I would like to thank you for the time you're taking to read and learn what is written here. You are entrusted with the minds of our children, it will be you, or a teacher like yourself that inspires the mind that discovers the cure for cancer, a new alternative fuel, or brings world peace.

–W. A. Gordon, Ph.D.
Integrative Behavioral Neuroscience
Functional Human Brain Research

Chair,
Advisory Committee
For Collection Concerns in Medicine
The David Geffen School of Medicine at UCLA.

Introduction

There are many excellent teachers out there with more knowledge and talent than I have. I have worked with some of these fantastic teachers and met many others on-line. Just because I have had the good fortune to work and communicate with some wonderfully supportive and helpful people doesn't mean everybody has had that same opportunity. It is my hope that the information contained within this book will serve as "the teacher next door" for those of you seeking answers to your daily classroom challenges.

There's no denying that times are tough, especially in the field of education. Teaching is a very difficult job, one of the toughest around. We endure long hours for low pay and receive very few, if any supplies and materials to do our jobs. If the information contained in this book can help make a teacher's job just a little bit easier then I have succeeded.

My first year teaching was spent in Seoul, South Korea. To say that I was lost would be an understatement. Not only was I in a foreign land where I didn't speak the language but the educational system was vastly different from what I was used to. With no mentor or support system in place, I struggled to find solutions to common problems involving classroom management, parent communication, and so much more.

When I returned to the U.S. and entered the world of public education I slowly started seeking out and discovering the answers to some of my questions. Each year I added more skills to my teaching repertoire. In 2001, when I first started sharing some of the teaching strategies and skills I had learned on my website, www.pre-kpages.com, I discovered there were many other teachers with the same questions.

Hopefully, this book will provide you with solutions to some of the challenges you face every day in the classroom. Most importantly, I hope it will allow you to spend more time enjoying your chosen profession and doing what you love best (working with young children!) instead of trying to reinvent the wheel.

I invite you to connect with me on Facebook, Twitter, and Pinterest for more early childhood information:

- www.facebook.com/prekpages

- twitter.com/prekpages

- pinterest.com/prekpages/

Vanessa Levin

www.pre-kpages.com

1
Facing An Empty Classroom

If your classroom appears to have few materials and furniture, don't panic. Before you spend any money out of your own pocket, it can never hurt to ask what, if any, budget money you will be given for your new classroom.

Often schools will provide you with basics like pens, staples, paper clips, stapler, tape dispenser, tape, and notepads so don't spend any money on office supplies until you find out what will be provided.

Many classrooms will have the basic furniture like desks and chairs; however, an overwhelming majority of new teachers can expect to receive little or nothing beyond the basics paid for by the school. Even in good economic times, this is a sad but common problem that many new teachers face each year in the U.S. If the answer to your budget question is less than encouraging, here are a few ideas detailing how you can gather inexpensive classroom items.

Books:

One of the first things most new teachers want to do is build their classroom libraries. Some of the best sources for cheap books are garage sales, thrift stores, and discount bookstores. Don't forget online sites like eBay and Craig's List.

Games & Puzzles:

Garage sales, thrift stores, eBay, and Craig's List are great for finding these types of items at rock bottom prices.

Tubs, storage bins, and caddies:

No Pre-K or Kindergarten classroom is complete without a wide variety of tubs, storage bins, or caddies for storing center materials or school supplies. The best places to buy these items are dollar stores. Most dollar stores carry primary colored bins, tubs, and caddies, especially at back to school time.

Chart Stand:

Be creative! Sometimes inexpensive household items can do double duty in the classroom. You can purchase a garment rack very inexpensively at your local superstore that will serve the same purpose as an expensive chart stand from one of the brand name teacher supply stores. No room for a chart stand? Try attaching your pocket charts to the wall with pushpins or staples. You can hang posters with skirt hangers. Attach a removable adhesive hook on the wall, place the hanger on the hook and you have an instant chart center.

Classroom Décor:

Another priority for new teachers is to purchase a wide variety of décor for their classrooms to make it stand out from the others and look attractive. For new teachers on a budget, try looking for items at thrift stores or garage sales that can be refurbished and given new life in your classroom. With little touch-ups here and there, old items can be made to look new again. A lamp can be spruced up with a new shade and chairs and end tables can be given fresh coats of paint (enlist friends and family if possible) to give them that special classroom look.

Grants:

Start writing on-line grants for classroom materials, technology, and furniture. There are several websites dedicated to helping teachers obtain materials for their classrooms, such as *www.donorschoose.org or www.digitalwish.com.*

Donation Tree:

Create a bulletin board outside your classroom featuring a tree. On the tree, place apple shapes with the names of the items you need written on them. Some examples of things teachers commonly ask for are: art supplies, office supplies not supplied by the school, games, puzzles, books, tissue, snacks, stickers etc. When a parent wants to donate something to your classroom he or she takes an apple. You can replace apples with new requests.

2
Room Arrangement

When you visit your new classroom for the first time, bring a notepad with you so you can write down what furniture and materials are currently in the room. Ask specifically if what you see will be yours. You may also want to take a camera with you to take pictures of the classroom layout and to remind yourself what materials were in the room in case they disappear before your next visit.

A tape measure will also be helpful when you visit your classroom for the first time. Take measurements of the room and other areas, and make note of all electrical outlets, computer hook-ups, doors, and windows.

Sketching a quick layout of the classroom on your notepad will come in handy later for room arrangement purposes. Once you have determined the layout of the classroom, the furniture, and materials that will be available to you, it will be much easier to arrange your room.

Armed with the sketches, pictures, and the list of classroom materials you compiled on your previous visit, you can now begin creating a floor plan for your new classroom. Most Pre-K and Kindergarten classrooms come with extra furniture for dramatic play areas and centers, so you will need to carefully design your floor plan to accommodate all the necessary centers and furniture. If you are unsure about what centers that you will need in your classroom check with other teachers in your grade level first. See Chapter 12.

The first thing to take into consideration when creating your floor plan is the placement of electrical outlets in the classroom. This will determine where your classroom computers, teacher computer, and any other devices that need electricity will need to be placed. Once you have determined where the electrical outlets are, you can begin working on other areas of the room.

Another important factor to consider when creating a floor plan for your classroom is the traffic pattern. Where are the doors located? When students enter the classroom where will they go to put their belongings away? Make sure that the area around the door isn't obstructed and there is plenty of room to enter and exit the classroom without tripping over furniture or materials. Providing a clear path from the doorway to the area where students will be storing their belongings is also important. Don't forget to provide enough room in front of the door for the entire class to line up so you can see every student. This will ensure a quick and easy arrival and dismissal time every day.

Once you have established where your electrical outlets and high traffic areas are you can begin visiting on-line websites that will assist you in creating a floor plan. Many websites now offer free classroom designer tools. These tools are user friendly and are very helpful when setting up any classroom.

To find free on-line classroom designer tools you will need to type the phrase "classroom designer" into a search engine. You will probably get several hits on your search so be prepared to visit a few sites to find the one that you are most comfortable using. The best thing about using an on-line classroom designer tool is that you can print out a finished floor plan and carry it with you to your classroom when you arrange the furniture.

3
Meet the Teacher

If at all possible, it is best to have some sort of "Meet the Teacher" or orientation type program before the first day of school so you can explain policies and procedures to the parents. At this meeting, it is important to have a list of things you want to talk about with the parents such as pick-up and drop-off procedures, behavior policies, lunch money, and snacks, etc. Having a list will help you remember the important points and make the meeting as brief and productive as possible. Also, providing the parents with a copy of your "Class Handbook" or orientation packet is extremely helpful. You could also present your handbook via a Power Point or Photo Story.

Parent Information Packet

Have a copy of your class handbook printed out for every student on your class list. Folders with brads in the middle work best and can usually be found on sale at office supply stores during back-to-school sales. On the inside front pocket place your "Welcome to Our Class" letter along with your business card. By using a three-hole punch, you can insert the class handbook in the middle of the folder, and secure it with brads. In the inside back pocket place other important information such as notes from the nurse, fundraiser information, or PTA membership forms. Make sure to have several extra packets prepared for late additions to your class and for those students who might move to the area during the school year.

Student Information

One of the most important things to do at an orientation or Meet the Teacher event is to gather information from the parents regarding how their child will be going home, and are there any food allergies or medical conditions you need to know about? Young children will not be able to provide you with this information. Therefore it is paramount that you gather it from their parents prior to the first day of school. The office may have already collected some of this information from the parents, but you may not have quick access to it on the very first day. This way, you will have all the information at your fingertips on the important first day.

Use a form that has the parents' names, phone numbers in case of emergency, food allergies, and transportation information and have them fill it out at the orientation. Do not let anybody leave without filling out the information form. These forms can be used all year for various purposes, you can three-hole punch them and place them in an "Emergency" folder that can be taken with you during fire or emergency drills or left with a substitute teacher when you are absent.

Instructions:

Step 1: Start by deciding which type of folder you will use to hold your Parent FAQ. I recommend the two pocket folders with brads but you can also follow the store sales to find the best deals or make your own folders (you can find directions for making your own two pocket folders here:

http://www.pre-kpages.com/summer-learning/

Step 2: Personalize your welcome letter, checklist, and Parent FAQs with details reflecting your school, grade, or program type. The checklist is to give to parents so they will be prepared for the beginning of the school year.

Step 3: Make copies of your finished Parent FAQ packets. I recommend that you make more copies than you will need so you can provide duplicates for parents who share custody. You will also want to have plenty of extra copies on hand for students who enroll later in the year. Make sure if you are using folders with brads that you select the three-hole punch feature on your copier.

Step 4: Create labels on your computer to place on the front of the folders. They might say, "Welcome to Mrs. Blank's Class" or something similar.

Step 5: Place your copies inside the folder and place the labels on the front. If you have two classes and want to have two different versions of your handbook for each group you might want to purchase two different colored folders to differentiate between the classes.

Step 6: Include your business card on the inside front pocket of your folders. You can also include a refrigerator magnet. You can order free business cards online at VistaPrint.com.

Extra Credit: Create a QR code and put it on the front of your packet so parents can save all of your contact info in their phones. At the time of publication the following service was free: *http://www.beqrious.com/generator*

Welcome to (Your Name Here) Class!

Dear _____ (grade level) Families:

This week your child will complete one of the most important milestones of his or her life - the first day of school! I am looking forward to a working with you and your children this year and helping them to achieve their full potential. Our days and weeks will be filled with many wonderful experiences and opportunities to learn and grow. We are so excited you will be part of our school family this year!

I would like to introduce myself, my name is _____, and I am delighted to be your child's teacher this year at _____ Elementary. This will be my _____ year with our school district and my _____ year teaching.*(if you're new don't include that last part, just say something about your family or hobbies)

I believe that a good parent-teacher relationship is necessary for maximum school success. Throughout the year I will communicate with you through notes, telephone calls, e-mail, report cards, and parent teacher conferences. You are welcome to visit our classroom at any time. I can always use an extra pair of hands and another smiling face when I am working with the children.

I encourage you to contact me if you have any questions or concerns at any time. You can call me at school _____ (phone number), send me a note, or an e-mail to: _____ You can also visit our class website at: _____ Our website has plenty of information about our classroom and school as well as links for you and your family to visit.

I am looking forward to a wonderful year with you and your child!

Love,

Mrs., Ms., Miss, or Mr. _____

Beginning of the Year Checklist

Are you ready for the first day of school?

- ☐ Lunch/Breakfast Money or Packed Lunch
- ☐ Backpack large enough to hold notebook (no wheels please)
- ☐ Extra Change of Clothes
- ☐ School Uniforms
- ☐ School Supplies
- ☐ Snack

Here are some examples of questions you will want to answer in your parent FAQ document:

Frequently Asked Questions for (Your Name Here) **Class**

What time does school start?

What time does school end?

Where do I pick up my child after school?

Is there an after school program my child can attend?

Can my child eat breakfast at school?

What if my child is late for school?

What is the attendance policy?

Will my child be eating lunch at school?

How do I pay for my child's breakfast or lunch?

What is the best way to contact the teacher?

Will my child bring home a weekly or daily folder?

Will my child have homework?

Will my child bring home a daily behavior report?

When will report cards be sent home?

What is the grading policy?

Should I send money to school with my child?

What if my child is sick?

What should my child wear to school?

Does my child need a backpack?

Does my child need an extra change of clothes?

Can my child ride the bus to school?

Do I need to purchase school supplies?

Can I bring a cake to school for my child's birthday?

What are the classroom rules?

What can I do to help my child at home?

What can I do to help the teacher?

How do I know my child is ready for school?

What are the school holiday/inclement weather notification policies?

Here are guidelines to help with answering each question.

1. What time does school start?

- (Insert time here)-students may enter the classroom.
- (Insert time here)-School begins
- Students are not permitted in the classroom before: (Insert time here)
- If your child is eating breakfast you may drop him or her off at (designate an area)
- It is the parent's responsibility to inform daycare providers of our class times, early dismissals, and holidays.

2. What time does school end?

- (Insert time here)-

3. Where do I pick up my child after school?

- Students are dismissed at (Insert time here)-at (designated a location), grades 1-5 are dismissed at (Insert time here) through (designate an area)

- If you will be picking your child up after school please be prompt.

- If your child will be walking home with an older sibling we will need a written permission note from you stating that this is o.k.

- Any changes to the way your child normally goes home will also need to be submitted in writing before they occur.

4. Is there an after school program my child can attend?

- Children who are (specify an age) may attend the after school program.

- If your child is (specified age) and you would like to enroll him or her in the after school program please go to the front office to request the paperwork.

5. Can my child eat breakfast at school?

- Yes, breakfast is served in the cafeteria daily before school.
- If you would like your child to eat breakfast at school it is best to be here no later than (specify a time) so your child will have time to eat breakfast before the first bell rings at (specify a time).
- The cafeteria stops serving breakfast at (specify a time) so please make sure your child is here in time to eat.

6. **What if my child is late for school?**

- We understand that there may be instances when it is not possible to be here on time. However, please make every effort to have your child at school on time so we can begin our day together.
- Tardies will be noted on report cards and habitual tardiness may affect your child's progress in (grade level).

7. **What is the attendance policy?**

- Regular, on-time attendance at school is vital to your child's success.

- Most of our learning activities take place in a large group setting and involve interaction with classmates.
- Many of our learning experiences take place in the first half of the day so it is important to be at school on time.
- After (state your school's policy) of consistent absence the school nurse or clerk will call your home to verify an illness.

8. Will my child be eating lunch at school? (If applicable)

- Yes, we will be serving lunch to all students in the cafeteria daily.
- All students are encouraged to eat independently; feeding of students is not permitted.
- Please do not ask teachers or other staff members to feed your child or force them to eat.

9. How do I pay for my child's breakfast or lunch?

- Parents are encouraged to go to the cafeteria and deposit money in their child's account when necessary.

- It is the parent's responsibility to pay for all meals in the cafeteria; please do not send any cafeteria money to the teacher.
- If your child receives free lunch then there is no need for you to deposit any money in their account.

10. How should I contact my child's teacher?

- All calls received during class time will go directly to voicemail; calls will be answered as soon as possible after school or during planning times.
- After school from (specify a time) I will be available to meet with you in person or take your calls.
- Of course, you may send a note to school with your child at any time in his or her B.E.A.R. Book, which stands for Bring Everything Always Ready.
- If you would like to schedule a conference to discuss your child's academic progress please feel free to call me at (insert phone number), e-mail, or send a note.

11. Will my child bring home a weekly or daily folder?

- YES: We will be sending home a B.E.A.R. Book.

- Please read the information in the B.E.A.R. Book every night.
- Every Friday we will send home a Pre-K newsletter titled (Insert your newsletter's name, e.g. "The Lion Cub") inside the B.E.A.R. Book, please make sure to read it carefully each week.
- Please make sure to return the B.E.A.R. Book to school every day, important information regarding your child's education will be included in the weekly newsletter and daily B.E.A.R. Book.
- We encourage reading the newsletter thoroughly and hanging it on your refrigerator for reference. The cost for replacing a lost B.E.A.R. Book is (Price); the cost for replacing the zippered pouch inside the book is (Price).

12. Will my child have homework?

- Your child will be bringing home a reading log in his or her B.E.A.R. Book each night.
- Please read to your child and have him or her record it on the reading log by coloring in one object. We will have a "Homework Help" night in

October where we will discuss other ways you can help your child at home.

13. Will my child bring home a daily behavior report?

- No, we will not be sending home a daily behavior report.
- If your child needs behavior interventions you will be contacted by telephone and a conference will be scheduled if necessary.

14. When will report cards be sent home?

- Report cards will be sent home (specify number of times) per year. We will notify you in advance so you can look in your child's B.E.A.R. Book for his/her report card.
- Please read your newsletter for the report card dates and instructions.
- When you receive the report card, remove and review it, then sign the envelope and return the empty envelope to school.

15. What is the grading policy?

- Students will be given grades of: (List your grading system here. e.g., *N – Needs improvement; P – Progressing; M – Mastery*)

16. Should I send money to school with my child?

- Please do not send loose money to school for ANY reason.

17. What if my child is sick?

- Please read the nurse's note carefully, it explains our health policy in detail.
- If your child is sent to school sick or becomes sick during school hours we will be contacting you to pick up your child.
- If you will not be sending your child to school due to illness please call the school and leave a message with the school office.
- When your child returns to school please send a note excusing him or her.
- ****IMPORTANT**** PLEASE KEEP ALL CONTACT PHONE NUMBERS CURRENT IN CASE OF EMERGENCY!!

18. What should my child wear to school

- Please send students to school in the school uniform.

  SHIRTS: (Provide the specifics, e.g. style, color, etc.)
- NO: (It is important to make parents aware of what type of clothing is not allowed.)
- PANTS: (Provide the specifics, e.g. style, color, etc.)
- SHOES: (Provide the specifics, e.g. style, color, etc.)
- NO: (It is important to make parents aware of what type of shoes are not allowed)

19. Does my child need a backpack?

- YES. All students will need a functional backpack large enough to hold a 9x12 inch notebook inside without folding or bending.
- Backpacks with wheels are NOT allowed, they are too cumbersome and impractical for young children to handle independently.
- Backpacks will be used daily for storage of extra clothes, so please make sure that your child brings his/her backpack each day.

- Many backpacks look alike; please label your child's backpack with his/her name visible on the outside.
- PLEASE MAKE SURE YOUR CHILD BRINGS A BACKPACK TO SCHOOL EVERY DAY
- TOYS, CANDY, and FOOD: For safety reasons please do not allow your child to bring any toys or candy to school.
- Toys can easily become broken, lost, or stolen. Teachers will not be responsible for toys brought to school.
- Candy and gum are not allowed at school at any time.

20. **Does my child need to bring a change of clothes to school?**

- YES: Please send an extra change of clothes to school enclosed in a Ziploc bag in your child's backpack as soon as possible
- **Please include the following items: Underwear, socks, shirt, pants or shorts**

- The change of clothes will be stored in your child's backpack – DO NOT REMOVE THE CHANGE OF CLOTHES.
- Because it is important for your child to have access to clean clothing in case of accidents or illness we ask that your child bring the backpack to school daily.

21. Can my child ride the bus?
- This will be a yes or no answer depending on your attendance zone and other variables. Your answer should be accompanied with an explanation as to why.

22. Do I need to purchase school supplies for my child?
- Again the answers here will be determined by the specifics of your school and your classroom. You also provide a reason why the parents do or don't need to purchase school supplies.

23. Can I bring treats to school for my child's birthday?
- Here you will need to explain the birthday protocol for your classroom. It is very

important that you and the parents are on the same page, because birthday celebrations are very important to most parents and all children. All children's birthday should be celebrated according to your protocol so that all children are treated equally.

24. **What are the classroom rules?**

- We try to keep the rules simple due to the age of the children:
  - Helping Hands
  - Listening Ears
  - Quiet Voices
  - Walking Feet
  - Eyes Looking

25. **What can I do at home to help my child be successful in school?**

- Please work with your child on the following skills at home:
  - Sharing
  - Cleaning up
  - Recognizing colors
  - Recognizing shapes

- o Recognizing/identifying numbers
- o Recognizing/identifying letters
- o Cutting with scissors
- o Buttoning, snapping, zipping, and tying

26. How do I know if my child is ready for school?

- You will know that your child is ready for school when:
    - o Your child can use the bathroom independently.
    - o Your child can dress him or herself.
    - o Your child can feed him or herself independently.
    - o Your child can separate from you without becoming overly upset.
    - o Your child knows how to wash his or her hands independently.
    - o Your child knows how to cover his or her sneeze.
    - o Your child knows how to wipe his or her nose independently.
    - o Your child follows simple directions.
    - o Your child can sit and listen to a story.

27. What can I do to help my child's teacher?

- There are many opportunities for parents to help the teachers and students both in and out of the classroom.
- We are always in need of parent volunteers to help in the classroom.
- If you are interested in helping please see your child's teacher.
- If you are unable to come to school to help but are interested in having projects sent home to cut or color, please let your teacher know

STUDENT INFORMATION		
Full Given Name:	*First:*	*Middle:*	*Last:*
Does the child use a nickname?		
Name We Should Use At School		
Date of Birth:		**Gender:**	□ Male □ Female
What language is spoken most often in your home?		
What language does your child speak most often?		
Has Physician diagnosed your child with a food allergy?		□ Yes □ No
If yes, please list any foods your child is allergic to:		
Medical conditions we should be aware of such as diabetes, asthma, or allergies?		□ Yes □ No
If yes, please list here:		
Student lives with:	□ Both Parents □ Mother □ Father □ Legal Guardian □Grandparents □ Parent & Step-Parent □ Foster Parent □ Other: _____
Who has custody?	□ Mother & Father □ Mother □ Father □ Legal Guardian □Grandparents □ Other:_____
How will your child go home from school?	□ School Bus □ Picked up in a car □ Walk with siblings □ Daycare Van □ Other:_____
At what time does your child normally go to bed?	
What are your child's favorite foods?	
What type of activities does your child enjoy?	
Do you have any family pets?	

41

4

Student Supplies

If your students bring school supplies you should be prepared to receive them in an organized and carefully planned manner. Having a large supply of paper grocery bags and a black marker handy is ideal for this purpose. As parents approach you with their child's supplies hand them a bag and a marker and tell them to put everything in the bag and write their child's first and last name on the outside of the bag. You can go through the bags later, sort the items, and mark off who brought what for your records.

Using a spreadsheet to record student supplies is always a good idea. This way you can track who brought what supplies in case somebody moves during the school year and asks for his or her supplies back. Make sure to have copies of the school supply list handy for those parents who have lost theirs or who forgot to bring supplies. As you begin to check off supplies write each student's name at the top of a supply list and highlight any items that are missing. Send the highlighted lists home with the students at the end of the first week if they haven't brought the missing items yet.

There are many schools of thought on managing student supplies. Some teachers prefer to have each child bring a plastic supply box or pouch and others prefer to have community supplies. If your students sit at individual desks then perhaps having individual supplies is best, if you have tables that seat several students then perhaps community supplies will work better for you.

Whatever method you choose, it is important to make sure your students have quick and easy access to their supplies at all times. When student supplies are not located in close proximity to their seats valuable learning time is lost as students travel to and from their seats to gather supplies.

Supply List

Teacher:_____

Student Name	Crayons	Kleenex	Glue	Scissors	Pencils	Red Folder	Blue Folder	White Paper	Color Paper	R B	Brown Bags
1											
2											
3											
4											
5											
6											
7											
8											
9											
10											
11											
12											
13											
14											
15											
16											
17											
18											
19											
20											
21											
22											

5
Cubbies & Backpacks

If your students have cubbies or a place to hang their coats and backpacks you will want to have all the cubbies labeled with the names of your students prior to the first day. If you ask parents to help their children find their cubbies, on the first day, it will free up a little time for you to circulate around the room and make sure things are running smoothly.

Another reason it's important to have cubbies or special spots labeled with student's names is to make them feel comfortable on their first day. Having a special spot for each child gives the child a sense of security and belonging that is very crucial for the first day of school.

When working with Pre-K or Kindergarten students, one can never assume that the children can recognize their own names. Therefore, using student pictures or a unique symbol in addition to printed names will help them identify their own cubby and prevent lost or misplaced belongings.

In addition to having names on cubbies, it is important for parents to label their child's backpack. There are some safety concerns about labeling backpacks with student names on the outside, but it is still important to have labels on the inside to prevent confusion. Many backpacks look alike, just like bags at the airport look alike. Therefore it is important to label them.

If you are concerned that your students may become lost without identification on the outside of their backpacks then you might consider a large, brightly colored, laminated shape attached to the outside of the backpack with your name and school contact information on the front. This way, if a child becomes lost he or she will be returned to you safely.

6

Name Tags

Will your students wear nametags on the first day of school to help you and the staff identify them? If so, you will want to have all the nametags prepared before the first day. It is helpful to distribute the nametags prior to the first day of school so students can be easily identified. See Chapter 3 for details about Meet the Teacher events. On the front of every nametag include the student's first and last name, how the student goes home- car, bus, walk, or daycare and bus number if applicable. If there is more than one teacher in your grade level it's best if you each select a different shape for your nametags so your students will be easily identifiable to staff when they arrive in the morning, during lunch, recess, or any other times of the day they might mingle. Of course, always have plenty of extra nametags handy for new additions to your class or for those that lose them.

It's also important to make sure your nametags are durable and can withstand the abuse of being worn by a young child for several days or even weeks. Creating a re-usable nametag will save you time in the long run, the trick is to make them out of something indestructible. The sticky name badges you can buy at office supply stores work well for adults, but they only stick to children for a few minutes before they become useless pieces of trash on the floor or stuck to the bottom of your shoe. If you must use cute shapes from the teacher store make sure they are made out of thick cardstock and laminated prior to use.

Another idea is to buy the colored, plastic folders at the office supply stores during the back-to-school sales and cut them up into nametag size shapes. Hole punch them at the top and attach using a piece of yarn or safety pin. Write student information on the nametags using a permanent marker or print out student information on address labels and adhere them to the nametags.

When you are adding student information to the nametags it's important that you write the student names in large, easy to read print in the center of the tag. Additional information such as room or bus number should be located away from the name in a consistent place on every nametag. For example, if your nametags are stars, the student name would be written in the middle, the bus number might be written on left arm of the star next to the word "bus", and the room number on the right next to the word "room".

7
Long Term Planning

It's important to have your year planned out in advance. This is alternately referred to as a curriculum map, a pacing guide, or scope and sequence. Think of putting your students on a bus and driving that bus with absolutely no destination in mind. That wouldn't make any sense. Therefore, before school starts it's important you map out your "route" so you and your students will end up where you need to be.

It is important to complete your long term plans before school begins- remember the kids are getting on the bus and you can't look at the map while you're driving.

Long-term plans are usually created as a group with the other members of your grade level. To begin the long term planning process you will need your national or state standards for your grade level, curriculum guides, school district calendars, school district guidelines or standards if applicable, and any textbooks you use. It is very helpful if you look at the end of the year requirements in each area first so you know where your students need to end up. You can then map out your year with those requirements in mind.

Creating your long-term plans in a spreadsheet is a great way to organize the information in an easy to read manner.

8

Lesson Plans

During the first week or two of school it is better to be over-prepared than under-prepared. Having detailed lesson plans written in advance for the first several weeks will help you establish a consistent routine. The first week or two in Pre-K or Kindergarten will make or break you. As a teacher, good planning is the key to success. Simply jotting a few notes on the back of a piece of scrap paper simply will not do. Having it "all in your head" is also not an effective lesson planning method. Even the most experienced teachers need to have good lesson plans in order to be successful. Every school district or organization has different rules and requirements when it comes to lesson plans, make sure to ask about these procedures before you begin creating yours.

It's important to have a good lesson plan template on your computer that is simple and easy to use. Principals, supervisors, and substitutes must also easily understand your lesson plans. Writing your lesson plans by hand is time consuming and not recommended unless your school or agency requires it.

Specific times and subjects should be listed in your plans as well as lesson objectives, descriptions of activities, book titles, and page numbers if applicable. In Pre-K and Kindergarten you should also include the titles of any music you will be using. CD track numbers and play lists if you use an iPod will also be helpful.

Lesson planning can be overwhelming, therefore it's important to know where to start. In addition to a long-term planning guide, which we discussed in the previous chapter, you should also have textbooks and possibly a specific curriculum to follow. Sit down with the teacher guides and look at the subject matter you will be covering in the weeks to come. If you don't have textbooks or curriculum to follow, research the state standards for your grade level on-line. Your colleagues are also great resources when it comes to lesson planning. Seek them out and ask for tips and advice on specific lessons.

Next, make a list of materials you need to gather. Books to read aloud are important for working with young children; make a list of the books you will need to find in advance. This may require a trip to the library. Once you have reviewed your teacher's guides and obtained your books, sit down and start filling out your lesson plan template. While you are filling out your lesson plan template, you may discover there are things you need to add to your materials list. After you have finished writing your lesson plans and adjusted your materials list, start gathering the materials you will need to teach your lessons.

If you are not the only teacher in your grade level then hopefully you will have a weekly team meeting where you can gain support and feedback from veteran teachers as well as gather ideas. During your team meeting make sure to ask specific questions about upcoming lessons and ask for tips and ideas for implementation. Many school districts also provide new teachers with a mentor. Make sure to ask if your school has a mentor program. If your school does not provide mentors you can seek one out on your own.

Consider asking another teacher in your building that you trust to be your mentor. You can also search teacher forums or the internet for mentors; teachers who have their own websites are usually willing to share.

A two-page lesson plan layout is included on the next two pages for you. Three-hole punch the first page on the right and place in a three-ring binder with the second page hole-punched on the left so both pages are displayed side by side.

	Insert Time	Insert Time	Insert Time
Monday		You can adjust column width to meet your needs Each week just "save as" using date or theme title so you don't have to re-invent the wheel.	
Tuesday			
Wednesday			
Thursday			
Friday			

You can type in things like recess, lunch, or specials here to save space	Insert Time	Insert Time	Insert Time	Insert Time

9
Substitute Lesson Plans

Preparing for a substitute can be a daunting task for any teacher, especially for those who teach young children. Teachers often decide not to call in sick when they should just to avoid preparing for a substitute because it's so time consuming. As a professional courtesy, you should always prepare lesson plans in advance for a substitute. Every school or organization has different requirements for calling in sick and leaving plans for a substitute. Make sure you are informed of the proper procedures for calling in sick prior to the first day of school just to be on the safe side.

When planning for a substitute it's important to place the lesson plans and all the materials the substitute will need in one central location. Some teachers label a tub or basket with the word "substitute" in large print and place it in a prominent location in the classroom so it can't be missed. Inside the container they place the necessary materials, lesson plans, and any additional information for the substitute in a clearly labeled binder.

Creating a binder filled with useful information for a substitute is part of your responsibility as a professional educator. In your binder you should include information such as a class list, a daily schedule, and classroom rules for your substitute in addition to lesson plans.

Keeping the information in your substitute binder current is also important. When you print your lesson plans each week, make an extra copy and place them in your substitute folder, just in case you are absent. Always update your class list and information in your substitute folder as soon as any changes are made.

One tip for preparing for a substitute in Pre-K or Kindergarten is to provide a page in your substitute folder with the names and pictures of each student. Pre-K and Kindergarten students are often shy around strangers and may not always say their names when asked; others may not be native English speakers or have speech impairments that will make understanding their names difficult. In these situations, having pictures and name labels available can be very useful for a substitute teacher.

Music is a very helpful tool when substituting in an early childhood classroom because of its ability to mesmerize and engage young children. Your substitutes will thank you if you leave them with a supply of songs your students are familiar with.

Create a substitute CD or play list on your iPod, fill the CD or play list with songs your students are familiar with and provide a book to go along with each song.

For example, place the song *"The Wheels on the Bus"* on your play list then include a copy of the book in the substitute container so the substitute can turn the pages and the students can sing along as the music plays. If you use a CD, add a small sticker to the back of each book with the track number written on it so the substitute will know which song to play.

The following is a list of documents to include in your sub folder:

- Class List
- Daily Schedule

- Contacts
- Behavior Expectations
- Lesson Plans *(www.pre-kpages.com/teacher-resources/)*
- Dismissal List
- Class Rules
- Emergency Procedures
- Notes Page for Substitute
- Map of School

These documents should be hole-punched and placed in a binder or folder in an area where the substitute teacher will be able to locate them easily.

10
Bulletin Boards
&
Classroom Decor

Before putting up any paper on the walls in your classroom or hallway, it is always best to ask about your school's fire safety policy first. Since 2001, insurance costs for schools have skyrocketed, requiring many schools to enforce stringent fire safety rules. Some of those newly enforced rules include limiting the amount of paper and decoration on the walls in school buildings. Once you have reviewed your school's fire safety policy you can begin putting up bulletin boards according to the policy.

The most important thing to display in any classroom is student work. Many new teachers expend a lot of energy on bulletin boards. However this is one area where "less is more". Instead of spending your valuable time changing out bulletin board borders and backgrounds each month, change out student work instead. Changing out student work frequently will keep your bulletin boards looking fresh and new.

Many teachers like to select a theme and or a color palette for their classroom. When every bulletin board display in the classroom has the same background and border, it is less visually distracting for young children and creates a more organized look.

Another way to keep your bulletin boards looking fresh is to use plain fabric or plastic tablecloths as backgrounds. These materials will not fade; they can also be re-used year after year. Stick to solid backgrounds and avoid those with a busy print, which can be visually distracting to your students.

11
Daily Schedule

Creating a daily schedule that works well for young children can be challenging. There are many factors that can influence your daily schedule.

Special activities such as art, music, physical education, library, recess, and lunch times are all factors you will need to take into consideration when creating a daily schedule.

You may have to wait for the students to arrive and then follow your schedule for a few days to know if it will really work or not. Often, a schedule that looks good on paper will end up not working at all, so be flexible and make adjustments if you notice something isn't working.

Because young children have very short attention spans it is important to balance your passive and active times throughout the day. When young children sit passively for too long they will become bored and start acting out; or worse yet, begin to dislike school. In order to hold their attention and maximize learning you must keep activities short and focused and balance the active and passive times. For example, if you start the day off with students gathered around for calendar time, you will need to provide them with something active afterward; such as songs and movement.

Another important part of a daily schedule in a Pre-K or Kindergarten classroom is the picture schedule. The purpose of a picture schedule is to provide young children with a sense of comfort by showing them, in pictures, the sequence of events for the day. When young children feel safe and secure in the classroom they will learn to love school and settle into the school routine more quickly.

The picture schedule is not simply wall decor; it is a learning tool that must be used consistently by the teacher in order to be effective. It works like this: each time you transition from one activity to the next you move a clip down the chart and announce that you are doing so.

For example, "It's time for calendar now; I'm going to move the clip down to the picture of the calendar." You may also want to appoint a helper who moves the clip when directed. Another tip is to sing a short song each time the clip is moved, this is sure to gain students' attention and help them transition quickly.

Here is an example of a song you can use:

Tune: Farmer in the Dell

It's calendar time!

It's calendar time!

Heigh-ho did you know?

It's calendar time!

Encourage students to clap along as they sing. This same song could be easily changed to fit each activity on the picture schedule.

The following is a sample half-day schedule.

Sample Half-Day Schedule
AM Class
- 7:50-8:10 Arrival
- 8:10-9:00 Literacy (includes read aloud, mini-lesson, independent reading, share, and small groups)
- 9:00-9:15 Morning Message

- 9:15-9:45 Writing (includes read aloud, mini-lesson, and independent or shared writing)
- 9:45-10:00 Recess
- 10:00-10:30 Math (includes calendar, read aloud, mini-lesson, independent practice/small groups)
- 10:30-11:00 Learning Centers (includes blocks, dramatic play, science, computers etc)
- 11:00 Dismissal

PM Class
- 12:10-1:00 Literacy (includes read aloud, mini-lesson, independent reading, share, and small groups)
- 1:00-1:15 Morning Message
- 1:15-1:45 Writing (includes read aloud, mini-lesson, and independent or shared writing)
- 1:45-2:00 Recess
- 2:00-2:30 Math (includes calendar, read aloud, mini-lesson, independent practice/small groups)
- 2:30-3:00 Learning Centers (includes blocks, dramatic play, science, computers etc)
- 3:00 Dismissal

Sample Full-Day Schedule
- 7:50-8:10 Arrival
- 8:10-8:15 Morning Announcements

- 8:15-8:25 Calendar Math
- 8:25-8:40 Morning Message
- 8:55-10:20 Literacy (includes read aloud, mini-lesson, independent reading, share, and small groups)
- 10:20-10:30 Bathroom break and prepare for lunch
- 10:30-11:00 Lunch
- 11:00-11:30 Recess
- 11:30-12:20 Specials (art, music, Physical Educations. etc)
- 12:25-12:35 Bathroom Break
- 12:40-1:30 Math (includes read aloud, mini-lesson, independent practice/small groups)
- 1:30-2:15 Writing (includes read aloud, mini-lesson, and independent or shared writing)
- 2:15-2:25 Snack
- 2:25-2:55 Learning Centers (includes blocks, dramatic play, science, computers etc)
- 2:55-3:10 Clean up and prepare for dismissal
- 3:10 Dismissal

Note: Music is integrated into all subjects as appropriate and therefore is not included as a separate block of time.

Note: Phonemic Awareness activities are integrated into all subjects as appropriate and therefore are not included as an individual block of time.

12
Centers

Centers are clearly defined areas in the classroom grouped by topic that offer materials and opportunities for hands-on learning. Research shows that young children learn best through engaging, hands-on activities; centers offer these types of opportunities. Centers provide opportunities for:

- ***Differentiation of the curriculum***
- ***Accommodating different learning styles***
- ***Independent practice***
- ***Small group work***

The benefits of providing centers in Pre-K and Kindergarten classrooms are many. When children are engaged in purposeful, hands-on learning there will be fewer behavior problems and more learning will take place. In addition, centers allow for self-regulation and are considered fun by children.

When children can make their own choices they feel empowered. If children are learning while having fun they will develop positive feelings about school that will carry on into the older grades.

TIPS FOR CENTER SUCCESS

Be Consistent:

Center names and locations should remain consistent to avoid confusion.

Hands-On:

Provide plenty of materials students can touch and manipulate such as magnetic letters and math manipulatives. Using materials that are 3-dimensional will increase student engagement and keep your students on-task for longer periods of time.

Reinforce:

Activities should reinforce skills that you have already taught your students. When the activities are familiar to students they will be more successful.

71

Demonstrate:

Show students how to do the center activities - telling is never enough.

Expectations:

Clearly state your expectations for behavior, noise level, and material usage. Never expect your students to know what to do even if it is late in the year.

Offer Choices:

Young children feel empowered when they can make choices.

Self-Regulation:

Helping children regulate their behavior is the key to school success. Self-regulation is a skill that is taught. It doesn't emerge naturally. If the classroom environment is responsive to their needs, children will learn to regulate their behaviors in school.

Centers offer opportunities for self-regulation. To create successful centers in your classroom, divide centers into four or five groups based on their proximity to each other in classroom.

Group centers that are near each other so the children assigned to those centers are not moving from one end of the classroom to the other to reach their centers. This will cut down on traffic and keep problem behaviors away from each other.

BENEFITS OF CENTERS

Science Center: The science center is a very high interest area. The items in this center encourage hands-on exploration.

ABC Center: ABC center should provide children with opportunities to explore literacy and letters.

Writing Center: In the writing center children are free to explore a wide variety of writing materials independently. The materials are readily available to the students and encourage creativity.

Puzzles & Games Center: Puzzles are important for developing critical thinking skills. Games promote cooperative learning and problem solving.

Play Dough Center: The play dough center promotes the development of fine motor skills. Make your own play dough with the recipe found here: www.pre-kpages.com/playdough_center/

Math Center: Materials in the math center encourage exploration and discovery; they can also promote the development of fine motor skills.

Dramatic Play Center: Important skills are learned in this center, such as socialization, peer interactions, problem solving, sharing, and oral language development.

Block Center: The block center promotes the development of fine and gross motor skills in addition to sharing and problem solving.

Listening Center: A listening center promotes vocabulary development, pre-reading, and listening skills.

Computer Center: A computer center promotes hand-eye coordination, math, and pre-reading skills in addition to basic computer skills.

Sand & Water Table: A sand and water center promotes the understanding of quantity, weight, and measurement in addition to fine motor skills.

Classroom Library Center: A classroom library advances pre-reading skills and concepts of print.

Flannel Board: A flannel board promotes oral language and re-telling of stories.

Pocket Charts: Pocket charts promote literacy, pre-reading, and math.

Dollhouse: A dollhouse promotes oral language development

Big Book Center: A big book center promotes a wide variety of literacy skills such as concepts of print.

Exactly when your students visit the centers in the classroom will depend on your schedule, full or half-day. There are many opportunities for students to go to learning centers in a full-day program. In a half-day program the opportunities must be strategically worked into your schedule. You can find pictures of classroom centers and lists of recommended materials for each at www.pre-kpages.com/classroom_photos/

13
Establishing Routines
&
Procedures

 Somebody once said that teaching Pre-K or Kindergarten is like herding kittens, and that statement is very accurate. The three simple steps below outline how you can establish successful routines and procedures in your classroom that will help set the tone for your entire school year.

Be Consistent

Following a well-planned schedule on a consistent basis will help you get off to a good start. Using a visual schedule that the children can see and manipulate is a big plus. Use a clothespin or some sort of clip to indicate what is happening in the classroom.

When it's time to transition to another activity give students a warning such as, "It's time for math in two minutes". When it is math time say "We are moving the clip to math time now". These types of clear, consistent transitions make children feel safe. When children feel safe they are more likely to have better behavior and follow directions more easily. See also Chapter 11, which details how to use a Daily Schedule.

Be firm but kind

New teachers are often afraid to establish good discipline in their classrooms because they worry their students won't like them. Actually, the opposite is true- being firm and consistent gives children a feeling of safety and as stated above, children need to feel safe at school in order to function properly. An example of a firm but kind response to a bad behavior is: "Johnny, I notice that you are throwing blocks. Throwing blocks is not safe. You might hurt someone. You can sit at the thinking table for two minutes now or at recess, it's your choice; what will it be?" No voices were raised, no lights were turned off, and no unkind words were exchanged, it's very firm but still very kind. Being firm but kind will help you establish a bond with your students and they will learn to respect and trust you. By being either too nice or too unkind you do not gain the respect or trust from your students necessary to be an effective teacher.

Music

Music is an extremely important part of every Pre-K or Kindergarten classroom. Using music in the classroom is one of the single most important daily routines you can implement; you can never use enough music. Have you heard the saying from that Kevin Costner movie, "If you build it, they will come?" The very same thing is true with music "If you sing, they will listen." The repetition that is heard in music is the type of repetition that children need to hear again and again to learn new concepts or reinforce routines.

Some examples of ways to use music in your classroom to engage your students are:

- Clean-Up Songs
- Good Morning Songs

- Good-Bye Songs
- Days Of The Week Song
- Months Of The Year Song
- Number Song, ABC Songs
- Leader Of The Day Song
- Basic Concept Songs: such as shapes, patterns, and colors, birthday songs, thematic songs (Old MacDonald during the farm unit)
- Lining Up Songs
- Going To Lunch Songs
- Walking In A Line Songs
- Washing Hands Songs
- Waiting Songs

A common misconception about using music in the early childhood classroom is that the teacher must have a good singing voice or enjoy singing in front of large groups of people. Neither of these is true, there is plenty of commercially made music out there that you can use in your classroom. There is no need to have a good singing voice because the children have no idea if you are a good singer or not.

14
The First Day

 One important thing to remember about Pre-K and Kindergarten children is that on the first day they will not walk in and sit down at their table or desk. Instead, they will want to wander about the room dumping out every toy or manipulative that you have available.

They may also bring their siblings on the first day, who can make an even greater mess than the students. One of the best ways to handle this is to beat them to the punch. Turn all of your shelves toward the walls or cover those that are stationary with butcher paper and tape them shut. You don't want all of your secrets unveiled in one fell swoop anyway. There's an element of mystery and anticipation if you put everything away and introduce things slowly in the beginning.

When the students enter the classroom on the first day it's important to have something for each student to do at the tables. Crayons and paper are a sure and safe bet for the first day. Put out blank paper and crayons and pre-date all of the papers. This way, once they are finished you can collect the papers and put them in the student's portfolios to show their very first attempts at drawing. Be prepared to have lots of paper available as Pre-K and Kindergarten students can draw one little scribble on a page and say "I'm done!"

If you are brave and put out toys for arrival on the first day be prepared for your students to do inappropriate things with them like throw them, put them in their mouth, or use in ways that they weren't intended to be used. It's best to save the toys for later when you can properly introduce them; you won't have time during arrival on the first day.

Another unique phenomenon of Pre-K and Kindergarten is that parents often want to stay the entire first day to make sure their "baby" is o.k. It's important to find out what your school's policy on this is prior to the first day of school. It may be something you want to mention at your Meet the Teacher night for example. Some schools do not allow parents to stay in the classroom on the first day as it can disrupt the establishment of a school routine and the formation of a bond between teacher and students. Other schools allow parents to stay which can lead to an even more stressful and crowded first day of school. Be prepared for whatever policy your school has in place and make adjustments to your schedule as necessary.

15
Introducing Centers

When it comes to center time, always remember that less is more. In the beginning of the year it is best to have very little out for the students, you can gradually put out more things as you introduce each center and the children learn the procedures and routines of center time. To establish center expectations properly in the beginning of the year, introduce only a few centers a day. Each center should have a set of rules that are reviewed each day at the beginning of center time for the first few months.

Spending time establishing rules for centers in the beginning of the year will significantly reduce behavior problems for the entire year. Never take for granted that your students know how to work with blocks, crayons, manipulatives, or any item appropriately. Many children have no prior experiences with the materials in a typical classroom. The rules of what is appropriate use of an object in their homes may vary greatly from what is deemed appropriate use in the classroom.

When introducing centers it is important to note that you should continue to review all the rules daily at each center for the first few weeks. Do this even after you have initially introduced them, and then periodically throughout the year if necessary, or when new students enter the classroom.

It's important not to overwhelm your students when introducing centers. Select just a few centers a day to introduce to your class in the beginning of the year. Introducing one or two centers per day in a half-day program and two to four per day in a full-day program is typically enough. This way you can gradually ease the students into the process of centers.

The following are suggestions for introducing centers:

Block Center:
1. Gather all the students and seat them in the block area on the floor.
2. Show them the blocks and say, "This is the block center" and refer to the center sign as a visual cue.
3. Pick up a block and ask the students what it is used for.
4. Say, "In the block center we use blocks to build things" and take several blocks to demonstrate how to build something carefully.
5. Take several blocks and give to one student and ask him or her to build something, clap and cheer when they are finished to show they did it correctly.

6. Show students how tall their structures can be (tip: use the shortest student in the class as a guide, nothing higher than that student's shoulders)

7. Ask students "Do we throw the blocks?" and model throwing for your ELL students. Use facial expressions or "thumbs down" to show that we should not throw blocks.

8. Ask students "Do we eat blocks/put blocks in our mouths?" and model eating a block for ELL students. Use facial expressions or "thumbs down" to show that we do not eat blocks.

9. Model how to clean up the blocks; show students where to put the blocks when they are finished.

10. Call two students to the front to clean up some blocks that you have placed on the floor. Cheer and clap when they clean up correctly. Use facial expressions or thumbs up to show that it was done correctly.

11. Pass out one block to each child and repeat the process above.

Play dough Center:

1. Gather the students and seat them in or near the play dough area on the floor. If your play dough area is too small you could do this in your large group/circle time area.

2. Show your students the play dough and say, "This is the play dough center" and refer to the center sign as a visual cue.

3. Pick up the play dough and ask the students what it is used for (tip: many may not know this one).

4. Say, "In the play dough center we use play dough to create things" and take a lump of play dough to demonstrate how to create something.

5. Ask, "Do we eat play dough?" (This step is VERY IMPORTANT!) Pretend to eat play dough and use facial expressions or thumbs down signal to show that we do not eat the play dough.

6. Discuss the consequences for eating play dough in your classroom.

7. Discuss how eating play dough may make you sick!

8. Demonstrate how to keep all the play dough on the table and not on the floor.

9. Demonstrate how to use cookie cutters, rolling pins, or other play dough tools you may have and how to put them away correctly.

10. Pass out small amounts of play dough to the students and allow them to manipulate it for a few minutes; use facial expressions or thumbs up to reinforce good behaviors.

Dramatic Play/Home Living Center:

1. Gather all the students and seat them in or near the Dramatic Play area on the floor.

2. Show students the Dramatic Play center and say, "This is the dramatic play center" and refer to the center sign as a visual cue. (Different teachers use different terminology when referring to this center, use whatever is comfortable for you and your students)

3. Say "In the Dramatic Play center we pretend."

4. Demonstrate how to play in the Dramatic Play center by taking out a few items such as a

baby doll, dishes, or pretend food and role-play.

5. Give your students a tour of the Dramatic Play center and show them all the things that are housed in that center and where they belong.

6. Pass out a few items from the Dramatic Play center to several students and ask them to put them away. Use facial expressions or thumbs up to show that clean up was done correctly; help those that are having difficulty.

7. Discuss the importance of not putting any dishes or pretend food in the mouth. Model inappropriate behavior and use facial expressions or thumbs down to show that we should not put dishes or play food in our mouths.

8. Introduce the baby doll(s) and demonstrate appropriate ways to play and talk with them. (This is very important as some students may act out physical violence or verbal abuse with the dolls) Say, "This is my baby, her name is _____. She's crying. I think she's hungry, I'm

going to give her a bottle." Act out feeding and carrying the baby appropriately and emphasize never hitting or yelling at the baby.

9. Pass a baby doll around to the students and have them take turns holding the baby doll and talking to it. Use facial expressions or thumbs up to reinforce good behaviors.

Book/Library Center:

1. Gather all the students and seat them in the book/library area on the floor.

2. Show them the books and say, "This is the book/library center" and refer to the center sign as a visual cue.

3. Pick up a book and ask the students what it is used for.

4. Say, "In the library center we read books" and take a book and demonstrate reading by holding a book in your lap and turning the pages gently by the corners.

5. Show the students the front of a book and say, "This is the front of a book". Pass books out to students and see if they can find the front of their books. Use facial expressions or thumbs

up to show that it was done correctly; help those that are having difficulty.

6. Show the students how to open their books, say, "This is how we open a book, carefully." Ask students to open their books gently and use facial expressions or thumbs up to show that it was done correctly; help those that are having difficulty.

7. Demonstrate how to turn the pages in a book, say "This is how we turn the pages in a book, by the corner." Ask students to turn the pages in their books gently by the corner. Use facial expressions or thumbs up to show that it was done correctly; help those that are having difficulty.

8. Demonstrate how to close the book correctly, say, "This is how we close our books, gently." Ask students to close their books gently and use facial expressions or thumbs up to show that it was done correctly; help those that are having difficulty.

9. Demonstrate how to return a book to its proper location, say, "This is how I put my book away, carefully." Ask students to return their books one or two at a time and use facial expressions or thumbs up to show that it was done correctly; help those that are having difficulty.

10. Ask students "Do we throw books?" and model throwing for your ELL students. Use facial expressions or thumbs down to show that we should not throw books.

11. Ask students "Do we eat books/put books in our mouths?" and model eating a book for ELL students. Use facial expressions or "thumbs down" to show that we do not eat books.

12. Show other inappropriate uses for books using the examples above as a guide.

16
Transitions

Transitions are the most difficult part of the day for any Kindergarten or Pre-K classroom. The key to making your transitions run smoothly is to model, model, and model. Never take it for granted that your students know how to "line up" or "walk quietly", you need to show them exactly what you mean and what it looks like.

TRANSITION TIPS

Lining Up

Model it! Pretend you are a student and walk to the line, place your hands behind your back (or wherever you want them to put their hands when they are walking) and then walk around the room quietly. Next, invite a few students to line up and walk with you while the rest of the class is watching, continue to walk around the room quietly in a line. Gradually add more students until the whole class is walking around the room in a nice straight line. Remember to give plenty of positive encouragement to those who are following directions.

Bathroom Procedures

If you must take whole class trips to the bathroom you will need something to keep your students busy while they are waiting for their turn. Keep index cards with short fingerplays or songs written on them with you and start singing softly with the children. Make sure to use plenty of hand gestures and movement as you sing to keep their interest levels high and take their mind off waiting their turn.

Cleaning Up

This is one of the most difficult transitions for any child to make. Never take it for granted that any child knows what you mean when you say the words "clean-up". He or she may have never heard those words at home, or they may have an entirely different understanding of what those words mean than you do. Again, it's always best to model how to clean up. Practice cleaning-up daily for the first few weeks, and then you will start to see the results you want.

Steps for a Successful Clean-Up

- Start by selecting your clean-up signal- either a bell or music will work well. Using a lights out signal is strongly discouraged as many children may find it frightening.

- Introduce your clean-up signal to the children *before* you introduce centers for the first time. Explain that when they hear this sound they need to stop what they are doing and put the toys away. Make sure to tell them what to do after they have cleaned-up; where do you want them to go now?

- Next you can show the class what "cleaning up" looks like to you. Select one student to come to the front with one tub of toys and model for the class. Sit down on the floor with the student and pretend to play with the toys. After a few moments play the clean-up signal and model for the entire class how to clean up and what to do when you are done. Celebrate a successful clean up with the class by clapping or cheering.

- Next, call two different students to play with the tub of toys, this time the teacher is an observer instead of a participant. When you play your clean-up signal make sure to celebrate a successful clean up with the class.

- Finally, allow the entire class to play in one small area with a few pre-selected items and practice cleaning-up using your signal after a few minutes. Celebrate a successful clean up.

17
Classroom Management

It is important to have visuals in an early childhood classroom as a reminder. You can make a rules chart using clip art and poster board. Post it on the wall in several locations in your classroom so you can refer to it when necessary. It is extremely important to keep all classroom rules positive. The word "don't" is not included in any of the rules.

How you introduce the rules to children is as important, if not more important, than the rules themselves. At the beginning of the year, on the very first day and every day thereafter, review the rules carefully as a group. Begin by asking the children "Does anybody know why we come to school?"

CLASSROOM RULES

Eyes Looking

Ears Listening

Mouth Quiet

Helping Hands

Sit Criss-Cross

After a few (usually incorrect) responses, prompt them by saying "We come to school to LEARN." Next, tell the students that learning is like "getting smart" (they usually understand that much better) and in order to learn we have to follow some rules. This is when you introduce the rules chart with pictures.

Tell them that there are five very important things they must do in order to learn. Then, say the rules out loud as you point to them on the chart. The next day when you ask these questions a few more students should be able to answer them. Finally, after several days, everybody should be able to answer the questions.

After the initial few weeks of this type of review, switch to having a child point to the rules on the chart. Have he or she say them for the class or pick friends to say each one. This process helps the children internalize and take ownership of the rules.

The book titled *Listening Time* works well at the beginning of the year during large group time. Read this book every day in the beginning of the year before every large group lesson. There are others in this series that address behaviors such as sharing, cleaning-up, kicking, hitting, biting, and unkind words.

There are specific methods of discipline for classroom management. One of the most commonly suggested is Love and Logic. Love and Logic works very well with the Pre-K and Kindergarten age group. However it does require patience.

Many new teachers may become frustrated and give up on Love and Logic too quickly. Love and Logic works by making the child responsible for his or her actions, thereby giving the child choices to make and then helping the child follow through.

Love and Logic may require minor adjustments to work with younger children, because many of the examples in the book are more compatible with older students.

One alternative to the time-out method is to have a "quiet area". If a child needs time away from the group he or she can go to the quiet area to help understand and regulate their emotions. Using a quiet area is more positive because it helps the child understand his or her emotions instead of just punishing the child for making poor choices. In the quiet area the child can learn how to problem solve and make better choices.

The items in our Quiet Area are:

- Soft stuffed animals for hugging if we are sad
- Books from the Best Behavior series (listed on pages 106-107)
- Wave bottle (has a very calming effect)
- No more tears magic sprinkles (empty decorative salt shaker)

You should avoid using punitive systems such as behavior charts, traffic lights, or ticket systems. These systems require a lot of work to keep up with and have many complicated rules. Be positive and work smarter, not harder. Moreover, research suggests, punitive systems have a very negative impact on the child's psyche.

None of the aforementioned systems hold the child accountable or have any flexibility. They are all or nothing. They are also very negative and lack privacy. It is demeaning for a child to have his ticket pulled and everybody to see that he has been "bad". What does that teach the child other than to be ashamed? Or maybe not get caught the next time? Acknowledging a child's good behavior is always far more powerful than acknowledging his bad behavior.

It is preferable to have a personal connection with a child and help him solve his problems by giving him choices and empowering him, these are valuable life lessons that a child will be able to internalize and use in daily life.

You should also avoid rewards, prize boxes, or treasure chests for the same previously mentioned reasons. Rewards and prize/treasure chests are expensive! It is much better to spend money on instructional items for the classroom and not flimsy trinkets that will become lost or broken within five seconds, often resulting in fights or tears. Also, what are we teaching children by giving them rewards when they "behave"?

They are being rewarded for doing something that they should be doing anyway. Knowing that they are behaving properly should be a sufficient reward in itself. The biggest reward they can receive is the gift of learning how to make their own choices and the good feelings that come with choosing to do what is right for the sake of doing the right thing. It is important to impress this upon them.

This does not mean you don't have a treasure chest in your classroom. Your treasure chest should not be used for behavior, but instead for special occasions, such as birthdays or other celebrations.

You can still have good classroom management skills without using behavior charts, tickets, stoplights, or prizes. Instead of using these items to promote good behavior, you should begin by establishing mutual respect, and then spend plenty of time modeling how to make good choices and role-playing different scenarios.

The modeling and role-playing is very time consuming but really pays off in the long run. If you want your students to share, then you have to invest the time in the beginning teaching them how to share. If you want your students to clean up on cue then you have to take the time to teach them how to do that as well. Teachers cannot take simple things for granted. Everything must be taught, modeled, and role-played with this age group to ensure success.

While it is preferable that your students like you, it is essential that they respect you. The best way to do this is by using techniques from the book *Conscious Discipline* by Dr. Becky Bailey to create a "School Family" where the students feel connected to one another and the teacher.

As sure as there will be rainy days, there will be times when you're trying to read a story and your students just can't sit and listen. Here's a good remedy for that. Before beginning any group activity such as a read aloud, review the rules first. You don't always have to use the rules chart, so it is good to have individual cards for the pocket chart using the same pictures you used for the poster and amend the rules a bit to fit with a read aloud.

These are a good set of read aloud rules: "Eyes on the reader, ears listening, hands in your lap, criss-cross applesauce, quiet as can be"

Hold up each card and you review each rule out loud as it is placed in the chart. This will eliminate most problems before they begin. Regrettably, the operative word is most. So, if anybody needs a reminder use a Love and Logic technique and say "Oh, how sad, I will continue reading when everybody is ready." Then put your book down and fall silent gazing into space quietly. This works like magic!

Don't give in and make eye contact, don't signal anybody out by name, just sit quietly. Soon they'll all be staring at you and you can begin reading again. In the beginning the pauses may be as long as 30 seconds to one minute, but soon they will only be a few seconds in length.

Consistency is the key with this technique, it may not work like magic the very first time you use it, but persistence pays off. This technique sure beats the old *"Be quiet!" "Stop it!" "Sit down!"* or in a worst-case scenario: *"If you don't behave we will be on the 6 o'clock news!"* technique.

RULES AND BEHAVIOR RESOURCES

The following resources are available at Amazon.com:

1. **Be Polite and Kind** – Cheri J. Meiners M.Ed
2. **Clean-up Time** – Elizabeth Verdick
3. **Feet Are Not For Kicking** – Elizabeth Verdick
4. **Hands Are Not For Hitting** – Martine Agassi Ph.D.
5. **I Love You Rituals** – Becky A. Bailey
6. **Know and Follow Rules** – Cheri J. Meiners M.Ed
7. **Listen and Learn** – Cheri J. Meiners M.Ed
8. **Listening Time** – Elizabeth Verdick
9. **Love and Logic Magic for Early Childhood:** – Jim Fay and Charles Fay
10. **Love and Logic Solutions for Kids with Special Needs** – David Funk
11. **Manners Time** – Elizabeth Verdick
12. **Practical Parenting from Birth to Six Years** – Charles Fay
13. **Share & Take Turns** – Cheri J. Meiners M.Ed
14. **Sharing Time** – Elizabeth Verdick
15. **Teaching With Love and Logic** – Jim Fay & David Funk
16. **Teeth Are Not For Biting** – Elizabeth Verdick
17. **When I Feel Angry** – Cornelia Maude Spelman
18. **When I Feel Sad** – Cornelia Maude Spelman
19. **When I Feel Scared** – Cornelia Maude Spelman

20. Words Are Not For Hurting – Elizabeth Verdick

21. You Can't Teach A Class You Can't Manage – Donna Whyte

18
Fire & Emergency Drills

Fire Drill Failures

Have you ever had a fire drill failure? Fire drills in any early childhood classroom are so chaotic it's difficult not to fail. Getting the kids out of the building at lightning speed is next to impossible, especially in the beginning of the year when they are becoming acclimated to classroom protocol and procedure. Mobilizing a group of four or five year olds is a difficult task at best. So, while fire drills are necessary safeguards against disaster, it doesn't make them any less stressful for teachers and kids.

Many years ago I worked for an early childhood program in New England. Those of you who live in colder climates know there is a law mandating that you open any and all windows whenever the temperature rises above 60 degrees. You also know that along with nice weather in the north comes the dreaded "construction season."

So, one fine day in May, there I was in my classroom with the windows open serving lunch with my assistant to our sixteen students. The ancient building that housed that program was in the process of having a new wing constructed – right outside my classroom window. The new wing would house the administrators of course, not the classrooms – that would make too much sense!

Picture this: the classroom windows open and the delightful sounds of backhoes and jackhammers going about their daily business, outside.

Suddenly, the school nurse burst into the classroom red-faced and ringing a miniature dinner bell. The only reason I knew it was ringing is because I saw her hand moving; the noise coming from outside the window was deafening. She was screaming, "We're having a fire drill and you're just sitting here! I've been ringing this bell for five minutes!" Now, you're probably wondering a few things:

1) Why is the nurse ringing a miniature dinner bell to signal a fire drill?

2) And why is she the one in charge of the fire drill?

The reason she was using a dinner bell is because the building we were housed in was older than play dough and didn't have a real fire alarm. (Yes, if not in violation of the fire codes, it is certainly dangerous.)

She was in charge of the fire drill because she was in charge of everything, and as the rappers say, "that's how she rolled back then."

Despite my explanations and the fact that the assistant didn't hear the bell either, the curiously over bearing nurse, insisted on writing me up for "failure to follow school policy", making this an official Fire Drill Fail. That's my Fire Drill Fail story. I'm sure you have yours. Here are some fixes to common Fire Drill Fail Stories.

Fire Drill Fixes

Every year there's always one teacher frantically trying to get his or her students to behave during a fire drill. Then there's the entire class that was caught off guard and is crying hysterically. The bottom line is that fire drills can be confusing and even terrifying for young children and as educators we need to make sure our students are prepared for them.

The following are some simple things you can do to ensure a successful fire drill experience for your Pre-K or Kindergarten students. You can avoid being *"that teacher"* by making sure both you and your students are well prepared for fire or emergency drills in advance.

Discuss:

Have a monthly discussion about fire and emergency drills and why they are important.

Read Books About Fire Drills:

There are several books written for this age group about fire drills.

Role Play:

Act out appropriate and inappropriate emergency and fire drill behaviors. Hold mock drills in the classroom to practice.

Wear A Brightly Colored Hat:

When the hallways are crowded with small children and adults it's difficult for little ones to follow you; a brightly colored hat will make you stand out from the crowd and prevent your students from getting lost. You can find cheap, colorful foam visors at your local craft store. Hang your hat on the wall next to your classroom door and grab it on your way out.

Provide Incentive:

Extrinsic rewards should be avoided in early childhood classrooms, however exceptions can be made in extreme circumstances such as fire drills. One type of reward is a "smelly" because in addition to smelling great, they are cost-effective. Buy a package of scented lip balm at your local dollar store and after a successful fire drill have your students place one hand on their head, then rub a small circle of scented lip balm on the back of each student's hand.

Emergency Drills

There are other emergency drills you will have to prepare for as a classroom teacher. Depending on what part of the world you are in you may need to practice for tornados, earthquakes, or other types of natural disasters. Schools in the U.S. are also required by law to have plans in place for emergencies that are not natural disasters.

All of these types of emergencies will require detailed planning and preparation in advance. It is important for teachers to know where to go and when. Therefore it is imperative that you familiarize yourself with the various systems your school or district has in place to deal with these types of emergencies.

Preparing young children for emergency situations can be a bit trickier. Some emergency drills require hiding under desks or tables; others will require you to be in a room with no windows and the lights off. It is important that the children are prepared for these types of situations in advance so they do not become traumatized.

Explain each drill to your students in very child friendly and simple terms so they do not become frightened. You will also want to inform parents about emergency drills by announcing them in your weekly newsletter or electronic communication.

Here is an example of what this message might look like: *"This week we practiced how to stay safe at school in case of a fire. Please take a moment to discuss the importance of fire safety with your child at home."*

Make sure you have an "emergency bag" stocked with a flashlight, tissues, and any other tools you might need in case of an emergency. Hang your emergency bag on a hook on the wall in an easy to reach location. A class list is also a must for any emergency drill. In the event of a building evacuation you will want to have contact information for each child readily available to you. Place current copies of your class list along with emergency contact information for each child in a folder and put it in your emergency bag.

19
Recess

Recess is no different from any other part of your classroom. You must model and show your students what your expectations are.

Recess Success

Have your students stand around each piece of playground equipment as you demonstrate exactly what is acceptable usage and what is unacceptable. For example, if you want them sliding down the slide only on their bottoms then demonstrate or have a child demonstrate for the whole class.

Make sure to let your students know the consequences for improper equipment usage.

After you are finished demonstrating each piece of equipment explain the playground boundaries. If your playground has certain areas where your students are not allowed to go, make it perfectly clear to them where they are allowed to go and where they are not allowed to go as well as the consequences.

Last but certainly not least, explain in detail what your line-up signal will be. Make sure the students are clear about what to do when they hear or see your line-up signal and what the consequences are for not lining-up.

20
Lunch & Snack

There are many unexpected pitfalls of lunch and snack at school. If you take your students to a cafeteria that serves meals you will need to teach them many skills in advance to have a successful cafeteria experience. Skills such as how to walk through the line, select their food, pay, and find their assigned table can often be overwhelming. If you are not well prepared in advance for the challenges the school cafeteria can pose it can quickly become chaotic.

You can avoid cafeteria catastrophes before they happen by taking a "field trip" to the cafeteria on the first day of school. Model and have the students practice all of the following skills:

- Walking in the hallway to the cafeteria
- Taking a tray and walking through the serving line
- Paying for their meal

- Finding the correct table or seat
- Opening milk and other containers independently
- Throwing away trash
- Exiting the cafeteria

The following are tips for teaching some of the steps above:

Walking in the halls:

Sing a quiet song and hold your hand in the air as you walk. The students will focus on your hand with their eyes and your voice with their ears and will be less distracted. This tactic is successful because it engages both the visual and auditory senses.

Taking a tray:

Your students will need to practice this several times. Walking with a tray in two hands is not something most young children have experience with. Balancing the tray so the drinks and food don't spill is even more difficult. You may be tempted to carry the trays for the children; however you should never do for a child what they can do for themselves. Independence is a skill that most young children take great pride in. Therefore, it is best to let them do it themselves.

Paying for their meal:

If you work in a federally subsidized program most of your students will not need hard currency to pay for their meals. They may have a number they need to give to the cashier, an identification card, or a badge to scan. Whatever the method used at your school make sure to teach your students to stop at the register and follow the procedure. Most young children do not have experience with paying for things, so this skill needs to be practiced in advance.

Finding the correct table or seat:

This seems like it would be the easiest part of the process but it can be the trickiest. Young children in motion are like trains, they are very difficult to stop in their tracks. The easiest way to get students to sit in a designated area of the cafeteria is to display an icon on the table at their eye level. If you have a class symbol like a star or a teddy bear put the symbol on a table tent and place it on the table at the child's eye level. Practice how to look for the sign and sit at the correct table.

Opening milk and other containers:

This skill will take time and patience. Young children often have great difficulty opening their milk due to their lack of fine motor skills. You will need to demonstrate and practice this skill with your class repeatedly over many days and weeks, for some children it may take all year to develop this skill. On the first day of school it is advisable to wear an apron to the cafeteria and stock the pockets with safety scissors so you can quickly help students open their straws, milk, condiments, and any other containers. If you have students who bring their own meals, stock your apron with a rubber grip to open stubborn thermoses.

Throwing away trash:

This seems like something all children should know how to do, but never take anything for granted. Teaching children how and when to throw trash away is the tricky part. Some children will want to get up every two seconds to throw away little bits and pieces of trash. Others will want to make basketball free throws from far away. Explain when it is appropriate to get up from their seat and how to throw their trash away.

Exiting the cafeteria:

This skill is one that must be practiced or chaos will reign. Show the students what to do when they are finished and where to go. If they are to wait at the table for a signal have them practice doing that. If they are supposed to walk to a designated area and line-up, then practice that. Model how they are supposed to wait- with quiet mouths or how they are supposed to get to the waiting area- walking.

Snacks can be just as tricky as lunch:

Will parents send in snacks for their own child each day or will each parent take a turn providing snacks for the whole class each week or month? Make sure to check with your program about regulations for snacks. Some federally funded programs do not allow parents to provide snacks.

It is important to communicate to parents at the beginning of the year how snacks in the classroom will work and how they will be provided. If parents are to provide snacks, then sending home a "snack calendar" with each child's assigned day or week will make it much easier. Don't forget to send a reminder home with each child when it is his or her turn. You will also want to provide a list of suggested snack items so parents will have some guidelines to follow. A suggested list is especially important if you have students with food allergies or families from other countries that are not familiar with the process.

If each parent provides their own child with snacks you may need specific guidelines such as no microwaveable snacks, junk food, or soda. If your students are bringing their own snacks you will also need to think about storing the snacks, do the students have enough space in their cubby to hold all their belongings and their snack? If not, where will you store their snacks? If parents send snack and lunch how will the students know which items to eat when? These are all questions that you will need to think about in advance to ensure a successful snack time.

Snack can be used as a tool to teach independence and also as a vehicle for teaching academic skills such as shapes, colors, sorting, counting, and patterning. Some snack crackers are even imprinted with letters of the alphabet!

Coffee filters can be used as individual snack baskets; they are very inexpensive and come in large quantities. Try to involve students as much as possible in the setting up process for snack. Some teachers like to offer snack as a center during free playtime. Students can visit the center and assemble their snack following simple picture directions. Whatever methods you choose for snack, make sure that the students understand the routines and procedures by modeling and practicing.

21
Parent Conferences
For
Pre-K & Kindergarten

Conducting parent teacher conferences can be overwhelming at first. It's important to establish goals for yourself during conferences so you can remain focused and on schedule. When it comes to parent conferences it is important to think about all of the following areas:

☐ **Scheduling**

☐ **Preparing**

☐ **Reminding**

☐ **Following Up**

SCHEDULING CONFERENCES

How to make it work for you:

- Scheduling can often be the most difficult part of the parent teacher conference process.

- Every school district has different rules. Some require that all conferences be done in one day, which can be exhausting for everybody involved.

- Others require that teachers fulfill their conference obligations on their own time, meaning after school.

- Regardless of how your district decides to handle conferences, you will still have to deal with scheduling headaches.

Here are some suggestions below:

If you see most of your student's parents on a daily basis, then using a sign-up sheet that offers a variety of different dates and times may work for you.

Send home a note or publish in your newsletter that the sign-up sheet will be posted outside of your classroom door beginning on a certain date and conference times will be available on a first come first serve basis.

Take the sign-up sheet to dismissal with you to catch any parents that might have missed it.

If you have any parents who did not sign-up, telephone them personally to remind them to sign-up.

If you do not see your student's parents regularly then you might want to consider sending home a note asking parents what dates and times are best for them to meet.

Create a sign-up sheet and keep it on your desk and as the notes are returned write the parents preferences on the sheet. Send home a note to those who responded to let them know the date and time that has been scheduled.

How to make it work for you:

If you teach in a school where it is difficult to get parents to come to conferences then a more direct approach may be required. Many parents will not come to school given the choice, so asking, "When would you like to meet for a conference?" is not an effective method for scheduling conferences.

It is important to note that parent teacher conferences are not the norm in many foreign countries and parents may have a fear of the unknown.

However, if parents feel that attending a conference with their child's teacher is a requirement, they may be more likely to attend. If you choose this approach it is best to know the work schedules of the parents (i.e. who works nights, who works 9-5 etc).

Create a sign-up sheet with the dates and times of all your available conferences and simply fill in the student's names according to what you know about the parent's work schedule. Send home a note to each parent letting them know the time and date of the scheduled conference.

If you are unable to schedule a parent for a conference after repeated attempts and methods of contact have failed then you may want to ask your principal if a phone conference is acceptable.

Some parents simply cannot or will not be able to meet for a conference with their child's teacher and they may be more comfortable speaking with you on the telephone.

Conference Forms

&

Notes

SIGN-UP SHEET NOTE

Dear _____ (grade level) Parents:
We are scheduling parent conferences for the month of
_____.

A sign-up sheet with available dates and times will be placed outside our
classroom door on_____ (insert date).

Please sign-up for a time that is most convenient for you.

At our conference we will discuss your child's progress in
_____
(Grade level) and review assessment data and work samples together.

Please plan to spend 20-25 minutes with me to review this information
and ask any questions you may have.

Please make every effort to attend the conference at your scheduled time.

SIGN-UP SHEET NOTE

Dear _____ (grade level) Parents:

We are scheduling parent conferences for the month of _____.
At our conference we will discuss your child's progress in _____ (grade level) and review assessment data and work samples together. Please plan to spend 20-25 minutes with me to review this information and ask any questions you may have.

Below you will find a list of times and dates to choose from, please select those that are the most convenient for you. You will be notified of your scheduled time and date after we have collected all of the responses.

Circle a day below that is most convenient for you:
Monday Tuesday Wednesday Thursday

Select 3 times that are most convenient for you:
Please mark your first choice with#1, your second choice with#2, and your third choice with #3.
3:15pm_____
3:30pm_____
3:45pm_____
4:00pm_____
4:15pm_____

Child's Name: _____

Please return this form to school by _____ (insert due date)

Thank You,
_____ (teacher name)
_____ (title e.g. Kindergarten Teacher or Pre-K Teacher)
_____ or _____
(school phone) (e-mail)

Dear _____ (grade level) Parents:

We are scheduling parent conferences for the month of _____.

Parent conferences are a time for us to meet together and discuss your child's progress in_____ (grade level). We will also review assessment data and work samples during this meeting. Please plan to spend 20-25 minutes with me in the classroom to review this important information and ask any questions you may have.

A conference for _____ (child's name) has been scheduled for:

_____, _____, _____
(day of week)   (month)   (date)

At _____ Room _____
      (time)   (location)

Please make every effort to attend the conference at your scheduled time. If you are unable to attend your conference at the scheduled time please contact me using the information provided below.

Thank You,

_____ (teacher name)

_____ (title, e.g. Kindergarten Teacher or Pre-K Teacher)

_____ or _____
    (school phone)   (e-mail)

CONFERENCE REMINDER E-MAIL

To:

From:

Subject: Conference Reminder for (student's name)

This is just a friendly reminder that we have a conference scheduled for _____ (date) at _____ (time) in _____ (location) to discuss _____'s (child's name) progress in _____ (grade level). If you're unable to attend please reply and let me know when you would like to reschedule.

Have a great day! (Insert electronic signature from your e-mail program that includes your contact info)

CONFERENCE REMINDER NOTE

A conference for _____ (child's name) is scheduled for:

_____, _____ _____, _____
(day of week)   (month)   (date)

At _____ Room _____
                (time)   (location)

Please make every effort to attend the conference at your scheduled time. If you are unable to attend your conference at the scheduled time please contact me using the information provided below.

Thank You,

_____ (teacher name)

_____ (title e.g. Kindergarten Teacher or Pre-K Teacher)

_____ or _____
(school phone)   (e-mail)

Missed Conference E-Mail

To:

From:

Subject: Rescheduling Conference for _____ (child's name)

I'm sorry you were unable to attend _____'s conferences yesterday at _____ (time). Please let me know which of the following days and times you are available to reschedule.

Monday _____ (date) at _____ (time), Tuesday _____ (date) at _____(time) or Wednesday _____ (date) at _____ (time)

I look forward to hearing from you soon,

(Insert electronic signature from your e-mail program that includes your contact info)

Missed Conference Note

Dear _____,

I am sorry you were unable to attend the conference that was scheduled for _____ _____ at_____ in_____
   (child's name)   (date)   (time)   (location

It is important that we meet to discuss your child's progress in _____ (grade level). I have the following times available to reschedule, please let me know which one will work best for you. Please check one and return to school with your child tomorrow.

☐Monday _____ (date) at _____ (time)

☐Tuesday _____ (date) at _____ (time)

☐Wednesday _____ (date) at _____ (time)

I look forward to hearing from you soon,

_____ (teacher name)

_____ (title e.g. Kindergarten Teacher or Pre-K Teacher)

_____ or _____
(school phone)   (e-mail)

135

GENERAL THANK YOU STATEMENT

Thank you to all the parents who attended conferences this month. If you were unable to attend your child's conference please contact me at your earliest convenience to reschedule.

Best,

_____ (teacher name)

_____ (title e.g. Kindergarten Teacher or Pre-K Teacher)

_____ or _____

(school phone)   (e-mail)

PERSONAL E-MAIL THANK YOU STATEMENT

Thank you for attending the conference for _____ (child's name) yesterday. I enjoyed speaking with you and learning more about _____ (child's name). I hope I was able to answer all of your questions, if you have any other questions please don't hesitate to contact me.

Have a great day!
(Insert electronic signature from your e-mail program that includes your contact info)

PREPARING FOR CONFERENCES

Organization

Having an organizational system in place before you begin your conferences is the best way to make sure everything goes smoothly. If possible, place all assessments, report cards, papers, or work samples that you want to review with the parents in individual file folders or "portfolios" for each student. This way you won't waste any valuable time looking for papers in several different locations. When it's time for a conference all you need to locate is one folder.

Conference Handouts

It is helpful to have several different types of handouts available to parents at your conferences.

Identify key areas that will be of the most help to the parents of your students and provide resources for them to take home.

Some of these key areas are:

- *Discipline For Young Children*
- *Bedtime*
- *How To Get Your Child To Listen*

137

- *Importance Of Reading Aloud To Your Child*
- *Development Milestones Of Early Literacy*
- *Developing Fine Motor Skills*
- *Practicing Math Skills At Home*
- *Practicing Literacy Skills At Home*

Print the handouts and have them organized in folders or on a table for quick access.

You can also make a folder for each parent that includes all the articles.

While you are talking with parents take out certain articles and highlight the information, which will be the most helpful for their child.

Conference Reminders

What may seem like an insignificant part of the conference process is actually one of the most important, reminders. Parents are very busy people and conference reminders are a must if you want them to show up.

Conference reminders don't need to be elaborate, hand-written notes, just short, simple, and to the point. It is best to send conference reminders home at least one day in advance if possible. You can send your reminders in the form of a note or an e-mail.

It's always best to start off every conference on a positive note before addressing any problems. Some positive conference starters for Pre-K and Kindergarten are:

- *I enjoy having _____ in my class. His or Her smile always brightens my day.*
- *I enjoy having _____ in my class. He or She is such a good friend to others.*
- *I enjoy having _____ in my class. He or She is so enthusiastic about learning.*

Follow these statements with a specific example to make them authentic.

If a parent jumps right in and asks you to address the problems say something like,

"We'll be talking about that soon, but first I'd like to ask you how _____ likes school."

This allows the parent to talk, but gives them a topic to talk about other than the problems. If they continue to insist say,

"It's important to me that all my students like school because this is only the beginning of their educational journey and I want to make sure it's a positive one."

Difficult Conferences

One of the most stressful aspects of conferences is sharing poor grades or assessments with parents.

Many teachers shy away from sharing bad news with parents or gloss over the facts, setting both the parents and child up for failure in the future.

When reviewing assessments or report cards with parents that show their child is struggling it is important to:

1. Show the parents examples of the child's work that reflects the reason for the poor grade. If the skill is not one that can be shown, for example concepts of print give examples orally and demonstrate for the parent if possible.

2. Tell the parents what skill the test or assessment is measuring and why it's important.

3. Explain how you are going to help their child achieve better results and how they can help you at home.

Here is an example below:

"Here are some samples of _____'s fine motor skills. This assessment tells us how strong the muscles in his hands are. The reason we assess this skill is because it is directly related to a child's ability to write. In the classroom we have multiple opportunities daily to exercise the muscles in our hands when we use play dough, cut with scissors, or pick up small manipulatives. I have a list of some activities you can do at home to help _____ with this skill as well. I'm sure with daily practice at school and at home that we can help _____ improve his fine motor skills. I'll give you the activities and review them with you before you go today."

Sticking to Your Schedule

Another challenging aspect of parent teacher conferences is staying on schedule. You do not want to make the parents who are waiting angry; this would not be a positive way to start a conference.

Many parents may have to take time off work to attend a conference so their time is at a premium. When it comes to parent conferences it's always best to move things along in a timely fashion to keep everybody happy. That is why it's so important to have an agenda of some sort before you start your conferences, even if it's only in your head.

If you state in your newsletter, e-mail, or a note home that each conference will require a certain amount of time it will help keep things on track. Place a small clock on the table in front of you so everybody will know what time it is.

After the initial introductions and formalities review any assessments, report cards, or portfolio samples before opening the meeting up for questions.

Missed Conference

There may be times when it's just not possible for a parent to attend a scheduled conference, and there will be other times when they just plain forget- we're all human. When a parent misses a scheduled conference it is important not to get angry, even if you stayed after school waiting forever.

Keep your cool and remain professional by calling, sending an e-mail, or note asking them to re-schedule. Give them a choice of times that are most convenient for you.

Conference Follow-Up

After all parent conferences are complete, a general "Thank You" statement made to all parents is recommended. This statement will serve two purposes, it will thank those who attended and also help you schedule conferences with parents who failed to show up previously. Thank you statements could be made in your weekly newsletter, e-mail, or note. You can also send personal thank-you notes or emails to each parent.

Documenting Conferences

Many schools require that you keep a written record of the parent conferences you conduct as well as proof of all attempts that were made for those that didn't attend. Included on the next page is a chart you can use to record your parent conferences. For parents that don't respond or refuse a conference simply write the word "refused" or "no response" across the date and time cells. In the column labeled "method" indicate if the conference was in person or via telephone.

Parent Teacher Conference Schedule

	Date	Time	Student	Method
1.				
2.				
3.				
4.				
5.				
6.				
7.				
8.				
9.				
10.				
11.				
12.				

22
Parent Communication: The Home Visit

Just as it takes a village to raise a child, it takes a village to successfully launch a child's educational journey.

Besides yourself and the child, the parents are the most vital members of your educational village. If you are going to be successful in launching your students on their educational journey, clear lines of communication with the parents are a must.

The following chapters will provide you with some useful tools to establish and maintain clear lines of communication with parents. In this chapter we discuss the home visit, which can make or break a good relationship between the parent and the teacher.

You begin with a home visit. A home visit is when the classroom teacher visits the home of his or her students. Home visits were first made popular in the U.S. by the Head Start program; however the idea has gained popularity in public schools, especially in areas serving at-risk families.

It is important to understand the purpose of home visits prior to conducting them. Home visits serve as a vehicle to open the lines of communication between the teacher and the family.

They are an important first step in establishing partnerships with families for the benefit of a child's educational experience.

There are multiple benefits to home visits. By conducting home visits teachers can:

1. *Reach families who may not come to school*
2. *Get to know the family*

3. *Work with families in their own setting, where they will most likely be more comfortable*

4. *Gain a better understanding of the family*

5. *Gain a better understanding of cultural dynamics (e.g. ethnic and religious practices)*

6. *Increase communication and trust*

7. *Increase student attendance rates and test scores*

Home visits can be used to:

➢ *Welcome new families*

➢ *Get families thoughts and opinions*

➢ *Understand families' goals for their child*

➢ *Answer questions*

➢ *Demonstrate learning activities parents can do at home*

➢ *Discuss ways the parent can help the child learn at home*

➢ *Get to know the talents and interests of students and parents*

➢ *Provide information about the program*

➢ *Reinforce positive parenting*

Home Visit Tips:

1. Never go alone, always bring your assistant teacher or another staff member along

2. Always carry a cell-phone.

3. Leave all valuables at home; only bring absolute necessities for the visit.

4. Leave your cell phone number and a schedule with your supervisor or other staff member listing the dates, times, and addresses of each home visit you will be conducting.

5. Let your supervisor or another staff member know when you will be returning or calling to check in.

6. If you will be conducting home visits in an area that is unsafe always call the police first, explain that you will be conducting home visits in certain areas and ask if there is anything you should be aware of before you begin your visits such as gang or drug related activity. If you feel unsafe going to certain areas request to meet the parents at an alternate location such as the local public library.

7. If a parent refuses a home visit suggest meeting at an alternate location such as the local public library.

8. If you are offered food always accept graciously, in some cultures it is considered rude to decline. Do not feel the need to eat all of the food you are offered, take a bite or two if possible to be polite.

9. Be culturally sensitive, in some cultures it is unacceptable to wear shoes into the home. Be observant; if you notice that family members are not wearing shoes, ask if you should remove yours before entering.

Home visits should last 20 to 30 minutes. If you feel a home visit may be taking too long, tell the parent that you have another appointment scheduled soon and you have to be on time in order to finish them all. If you feel that you may be in danger don't hesitate to cut the visit short and report the incident immediately to your supervisor or call 9-1-1 if the situation is life threatening.

How often you conduct home visits may depend on your program or agency; but generally speaking, home visits are usually conducted at least twice a year, once before school starts and again towards the end of the school year.

During a home visit you should be meeting with and getting to know the parent as well as the child. See specific ideas for fun activities beginning on page 152.

Some ideas for meeting with the parents include:

1. Introduce yourself to the parents and child to put them at ease.
2. Provide the child with a fun activity.
3. Provide a little background information about yourself such as how long you have been teaching and perhaps some general personal information such as your hobbies or how many children or pets you have.
4. Have parents fill out any forms you may require or ask them the questions and you will fill them out as they respond. How you approach this task may

depend on whether the parents are literate or not. It's important to be aware and sensitive to the possibility that you may need to be the one to fill out the form.

5. Provide and review orally with parents a class handbook answering basic program information such as the times class will start and end or transportation arrangements in addition to frequently asked questions.

6. Provide parents with your school contact information.

7. Ask parents if they have questions.

8. Ask parents for permission to take a picture of the family. Make sure you explain the reason you are asking. You will need to bring a digital camera or use your phone if it has a camera feature.

9. Ask parents for permission to take a picture of the student. Make sure you explain the reason you are asking. You will need to bring a digital camera or use your phone if it has a camera feature.

BREAKING THE ICE WITH FUN ACTIVITIES

Another important aspect of any home visit is connecting with the student. It is crucial that you form a bond with the child when you visit the home. This will help erase the fear of the unknown and ease separation anxiety on the first day. When children feel comfortable and know the teacher in advance they are less likely to become anxious and cry on the first day of school.

When you show an interest in the child and make an effort to bond you are also showing the parent that you are a person who can be trusted to care for their child. Parent's attitudes about school and the teacher can easily be communicated to the child through body language; when the parents are at ease and have positive attitudes then the child will respond in kind. Below you will find several activities to help you break the ice and get to know your students better:

Gift Bags:

Purchase a set of white paper lunch bags from the store. Fill each bag with a few simple and inexpensive items such as homemade crayons (see recipe below), one or two special pencils, stickers, a granola bar or other healthy, kid friendly snack, and a trinket or two from the dollar store or Oriental Trading.

Decorate the outside of the lunch bags by stamping them with ink stamps or decorating with stickers. Attach a personal note to the top of the bag welcoming the student to your class and include a picture of yourself if possible.

Books:

This activity can be done two different ways:

If you have a Scholastic account, order one $1 book in advance for every child using your bonus points. Or, go to the library and check out several books that you will be reading to your class the first week of school.

Very popular titles such as *Chicka, Chicka Boom Boom! Brown Bear, Brown Bear, What Do You See? No David!* or *The Kissing Hand* are all good choices.

When you visit each child's home, read one book to him or her, then take one picture of the child holding that book. Next, take another picture with the child, parent(s), and any siblings sitting together looking at the book.

Pictures:

Use the pictures you took of the students and their families to create bulletin boards and class books so students will feel welcome on the first day.

One example of a bulletin board is titled "Caught Reading" featuring the pictures of the students reading with their families. Decorate the board with a bug border, bug accents, and a bug catching net or fly swatters.

Another example of a bulletin board you can create using student pictures is titled *"Chicka Chicka Boom Boom Look Who Likes to Read in Our Room!"* Decorate the board with palm trees, colorful borders, background, and letters.

You could do the same thing using the book Brown Bear, Brown Bear, What Do You See? Title the board "Mrs.____'s Class, Mrs. ____'s Class What Do You See?" and have pictures of each student holding the Brown Bear Book captioned with "I see _____ (child's name) looking at me."

You can also create a class book using the ideas above and send the book home with a different student each night so students can learn the names of their classmates.

You could also use the book *Brown Bear Brown Bear What Do You See?* and student pictures to create a class book.

Paper:

Never underestimate the power of plain paper. Using the homemade crayons from the gift bag, encourage each child to draw a picture on a blank piece of white paper. White paper looks best on bulletin boards and makes the child's work stand out.

Create a bulletin board with a solid background and bright border in your classroom or hallway featuring the pictures the students made during the home visit. Having their work on the wall will show them that you value and respect them as learners, help them feel at home in their new classroom, and ease anxiety.

Melted Crayon Recipe:

1. Purchase inexpensive, plastic candy molds at the craft store in fun shapes or favorite characters. You can also use the soft, rubber ice cube trays that come in different shapes.

2. Enlist children and volunteers to help you peel old crayons

3. Break the crayons into small pieces

4. Spray the candy mold or ice cube tray lightly with non-stick spray

5. Place the crayons in a disposable container and melt in the microwave

6. Pour the melted crayons into the candy molds or ice cube trays and let cool

Home Visit Schedule

	Student	Parent	Time	Address	Phone
1					
2					
3					
4					
5					
6					
7					
8					
9					
10					
11					
12					

STUDENT PROFILE_____

Level of Concern	None	Some	Great	Comments
Is active				
Tires easily				
Plays with other children				
Listens to parents				
Gets along with others				
Gets along with adults				
Expresses self orally				
Speech is easily understood				
Accepts changes in routine				
Has to be disciplined often				
Follows simple oral directions				
Dresses and feeds self independently				
Cries easily				
Has temper tantrums				
Fights with other children				

3 Stars and a Wish

The purpose of the 3 Stars and a Wish form on the following page is to show parents that you value and respect their input. The information collected from this form can be used in various ways.

You can create a bulletin board featuring the family photos with one "star" statement printed below for each child. Another way is to place the form in the child's portfolio and discuss the comments with parents during conferences.

You can use this document as a springboard to share your observations of the child with the parents and follow up with 3 stars and a wish of your own for the child.

3 Stars and a Wish Directions

In the spaces provided below please list three things about your child that are "star quality" and make you proud, for example "I am proud of my child because she always says please and thank you."

Add a wish for your child at the bottom, a wish can be the one thing you most want your child to learn in our class this year or a broader goal such as going to college.

Return this paper to your child's teacher in the envelope provided on the first day of school.

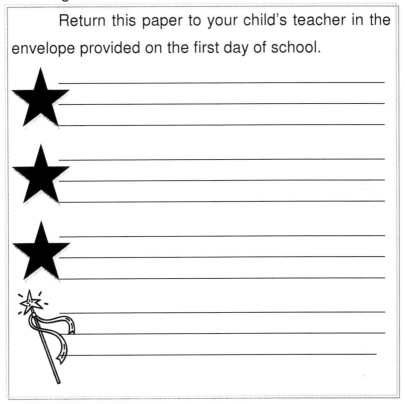

23
Parent Communication:
Other Tools

Buddy Bags are designed to be fun and informative ways for families to share literacy and learning experiences at home. A Book Buddy is a stuffed animal or character that goes home in a special backpack with one student along with books and activities.

One Buddy Bag is sent home with a different child each day. The bags are distributed on a rotating basis so each child will have a turn numerous times throughout the school year. Families will read the book(s) and participate in the activities. The Buddy Bag is to be returned to school the next day.

Buddy Bags go home with one child in each class, each day. Thus, if you have two classes, you will have two bags checked out each night. So, make it habit to check that two bags have been returned at the beginning of each class.

Clear backpacks work best because they can withstand the wear and tear associated with young children and are easy to clean.

Some examples of Buddy Bag contents are listed below.

It is advisable to have parents sign a contract to participate in the Buddy Bag program. Inside each bag there is a note that is printed on cardstock and laminated that explains what is in the bag and how to use it.

Creating Buddy Bags doesn't have to break the bank. You can easily find items to stock the bags at discount stores, garage sales, and thrift stores.

Buddy Bags can be created to reinforce skills that you have taught in the classroom. You can create Buddy Bags for:

- Nursery Rhymes

- Fairy Tales
- Birthday Celebrations

You can create Buddy bags to go with popular books such as:

- *Chicka Chicka Boom Boom* by Bill Martin Jr., John Archambault and Lois Ehlert
- *Brown Bear, Brown Bear. What Do You See?* by Bill Martin Jr. and Eric Carle
- *Goodnight Moon* by Margaret Wise Brown
- *Clifford* by Norman Bridwell
- *No David!* by David Shannon

You can also create Buddy Bags to go with units of study such as:

- Plants and seeds
- Weather
- Fire safety
- Farm
- Seasons
- Transportation

Items to consider including in Buddy Bags:

Instruction sheet for parents:

- One or more books to go with the topic

- Stuffed companion character or animal
- One puzzle or activity to with the theme
- Story recorded on CD or iPod

BUDDY BAG PRINTABLES: LEADER BACKPACK

PLEASE RETURN THE BACKPACK AND ALL CONTENTS TO SCHOOL TOMORROW.

Dear Family:

Your child is bringing home the _____ Backpack today. Ask your child what types of special things he/she did at school today.

Please read the book(s) in the backpack to your child. There may be other activities such as flash cards, games, or puzzles included along with the book. Please help your child complete any other activities that are included in the backpack.

Please return all the contents of the backpack in the same condition that you received them.

Please keep the backpack and all contents safe from younger siblings and pets.

There is a list of contents on the back of this note; please check the list to make sure everything is in the bag.

Thank you for your cooperation and have a wonderful evening!

BUDDY BAG CONTRACT

Dear Pre-K Families:

Our class has many "Buddy Bags" that go home on a rotating basis. A Buddy Bag is a special backpack that may contain activities, books and a stuffed animal or character that goes home with our class leader each day.

Buddy Bags are designed to be fun and informative ways for families to share literacy and learning experiences at home. Buddy Bags are a way to connect our school family with your home family in meaningful and enjoyable ways. The bags may contain specific theme related books and materials for you to enjoy at home with your child. Some bags are for special occasions such as birthdays and others are to reinforce things we are learning about in class.

Please discuss with your child the importance of being responsible and taking good care of the bag when it is their turn. Because the bags are expensive and some items may be difficult to replace we are asking that you sign this form to participate in the Buddy Bag project. If you and your child would like to participate in our Buddy Bag project please sign and return this form to school with your child.

Thank you for your interest

____ YES

We would like to participate in the Buddy Bag project. We understand that the Buddy Bags need special care and responsibility and we will do our best to care for them.

Child's name: _____

Parent Signature:_____

B.E.A.R. Books

Bring Everything Always Ready

B.E.A.R. Books are one-inch three-ring binders that are used as a daily method of communication between home and school. B.E.A.R. stands for Bring Everything Always Ready". "Clear View" binders allow you to slip in a cover page that will last all year. Make sure to include the student's name, school address, and phone-number on the cover page in case the book is lost.

The best place to buy binders is at warehouses, such as Sam's Club or Costco where you can purchase them in bulk.

Using B.E.A.R. Books helps maintain effective communication between home and school. B.E.A.R. Books also help eliminate lost papers and messy backpacks. In general, the notebooks teach necessary organizational skills to children at an early age and help the parent stay organized at the same time.

Often, if parents have more than one child it is difficult to keep up with all the notes, papers, and homework that are sent home on a daily basis, B.E.A.R. helps with this problem.

B.E.A.R. Books can contain various items according to your needs:

- A zippered pouch to hold money that is sent to school for lunch, field trips, Scholastic book orders etc.
- Welcome Letter explaining the purpose of the B.E.A.R. Book and how it all works.
- Weekly Newsletter
- Copy of your class list
- Reading Log for parents to sign nightly.
- Monthly Calendar
- School year calendar with dates of all school holidays and important events.
- Skill sheets, such as charts of ABC's, numbers, colors, and shapes for homework practice; print on cardstock, laminate for durability, and three-hole punch.
- A pencil in the zippered pouch, so parents always have something to write with.

- Blank notebook paper in the back for parent/teacher communication. Parents can write notes to and from school, or the teacher can write notes to the parent.
- Behavior sheet if you choose to use one.

It is best to look at the B.E.A.R. Books first thing in the morning because you never know what will happen the rest of the day, you may end up not having enough time later. It only takes a few minutes once you get used to it and know exactly where to check for notes, money etc. If you have an assistant, this is something he or she can help with.

Here are some other acronyms for B.E.A.R. Books

- Becoming Efficient (or Effective) And Responsible
- Being Excited About Responsibility

There are several options for funding B.E.A.R. Books. If you work in a federally subsidized program there are certain funds that are allocated for parent communication, ask if you can use those funds to purchase your B.E.A.R. Books.

Another option is to put the notebook and zipper pouch on your supply list and have the parents purchase it. However, this is not an option for everybody and some teachers have had success in asking for local businesses to pay for B.E.A.R. Books. "Where there's a will there's a way."

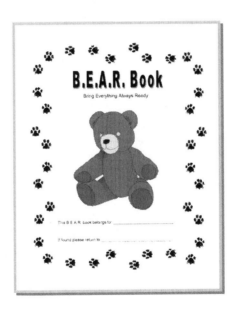

B.E.A.R. Book Letter to Parents

Welcome to our B.E.A.R. Book! B.E.A.R. stands for Bring Everything Always Ready. B.E.A.R. Books are a great way for us to share information about what is happening at school and at home.

In the front of the B.E.A.R. Book you will see a clear zippered pouch; this pouch is for sending money to and from school if necessary and it will also contain your child's homework cards at a later date. The replacement cost for the zippered pouch is $1

Our weekly newsletter will be placed in the B.E.A.R. Book every Friday, please read the newsletter carefully for important information about upcoming events, important announcements, and much more. You may remove the newsletter from the book or you may leave it in the folder if you wish.

Lined paper is included in the back of the B.E.A.R. Book for your convenience. If you need to send me a note for any reason you may use this paper to write on. There is a pencil in the zippered pouch if you need something to write with, please leave it in the pouch.

Please check the inside front pocket of your child's B.E.A.R. Book for important notes from the teacher or office every day. Notes in the inside front pocket are to be removed each night.

Please return the B.E.A.R. Book to school every day in your child's backpack.

Please keep the B.E.A.R. Book and all the contents safe from food, drinks, younger siblings, and pets.

Please do not allow your child to color or write in or on the B.E.A.R. Book.

These useful resources are available from *amazon.com* and in some book stores.

1. TY Babie Beanies - Yummy - Gingerbread Man –Ty Babie Beanies - Yummy - Gingerbread Man
2. Humpty Dumpty Plush Toy by Scholastic Sidekicks Makes a Musical Jingling Sound When Shaken – Sidekicks
3. NO DAVID PLUSH DOLL Character by David Shannon – Yottoy
4. How do Dinosaurs Say Good Night? 14" – Merry Makers
5. Manhattan Toy Dr. Seuss Cat in the Hat – Small
6. The Very Hungry Caterpillar Board Book and Plush (Book &Toy) [Board Book] – Eric Carle
7. The World of Eric Carle Brown Bear Plush By Kids Preferred – Kids Preferred
8. The World of Eric Carle Polar Bear Plush by Kids Preferred – Kids Preferred
9. The World of Eric Carle Panda Bear Plush by Kids Preferred – Kids Preferred
10. The World of Eric Carle Brown Bear Bean Bag Toy by Kids Preferred – Kids Preferred
11. The World of Eric Carle Elephant Bean Bag Toy by Kids Preferred – Kids Preferred
12. The World of Eric Carle Very Grouchy Ladybug Bean Bag Toy by Kids Preferred – Kids Preferred
13. Goodnight Moon Rabbit Plush, 7" – Crocodile Creek
14. Home And Back With Books: 60 Take-Home Activities for Family Fun Grades K-1 [Paperback] – Kimberley Jordano, Author; Joel Kupperstein, Editor
15. Idea Bags: Activities to Promote the School to Home Connection Prek-1 (Fearon Teacher Aid Book) [Paperback] – Sharon McDonald, Author; Corbin Hillam, Illustrator

24
ESL:
English as a Second Language

One of the most common misconceptions is that you will have to stop and change the way you do everything if you get an ESL student. Nothing could be further from the truth. As early childhood educators almost everything we do in the classroom daily is conducive to learning the English language.

You must remember that to young children the entire world is new. They are learning new words every day. So if you tell them apple is a word for apple, and that *manzana* and *pomme* are also words for apple, they will most likely say, "okay", and go back to the play dough. Adults concern themselves with speaking and learning different languages. Children just concern themselves with speaking and learning.

Below you will find information and tips that will lay your fears to rest and make your ESL students feel safe and comfortable in their new classroom.

Use hand gestures and facial expressions to communicate with a child who doesn't speak English. You will be surprised at how much you can convey with these alone. Just like any other young child, ESL students will also pick up on your body language so be relaxed and confident, smile often, and give the thumbs up sign when things are going well. Speak clearly, enunciate your words, and avoid use of regional slang or colloquialisms.

Try to provide visuals and props whenever possible to help your ESL students better understand a concept. For example, your class rules can be made with pictures. Whenever you sing a song you can also try to have a prop or puppet, for example if you sing the song *Five Green Speckled Frogs,* you would have five frog props (stuffed animal type or puppets) to help your ESL students.

You should also provide a thematic word wall for each of your units of study with pictures of each word and lots of hands on learning with manipulatives whenever possible to strengthen understanding.

Teachers often mistakenly believe they have to speak the native language of the ESL student. An ESL teacher is an English teacher. ESL teachers do not need to speak the student's native language to teach English. As an ESL teacher you will often have students who speak several different languages in your classroom at the same time and there is no way you could master all those languages in order to teach them English.

Don't panic if your ESL students don't talk at first. It doesn't mean that they are not learning; it doesn't mean that you need to do anything differently. Nothing is wrong. Most ESL students will go through a "silent period" that lasts anywhere from six weeks to three months, or even an entire school year. During this time the ESL student(s) are absorbing their new language and are often afraid of speaking and making a mistake.

It's very important that the teacher or peers do not force ESL students to speak during this time or punish them for not speaking, however lots of praise and encouragement often works wonders. You should entice your ESL students into speaking through the use of props and music. What four year old doesn't love speaking into a microphone and hearing his or her voice, or singing along to a song with big alligator puppet? By making English less scary and more fun, your ESL students will often be talking a blue streak by the end of the year.

You might find you have several ESL students who all speak the same language and they are always talking to each other in their native language. Your instinct might be to think: how can they learn if they don't speak English in my class? You should never discourage your students from using their native language in the classroom or at home.

Often ESL students will discuss concepts they are learning in your classroom in their native language, thus helping them gain comprehension. You don't want English to replace their native language; you want them to learn English as a Second Language. Banning their native language in the classroom will force ESL students to lose their cultural identity and feel "bad" for speaking their native language, thus feeling bad about themselves and their culture. Sometimes parents mistakenly think that they are helping their children by banning their native language in the home, forcing them to speak English only. However, this only results in children who have no native language or cultural identity, which will negatively affect their self-esteem and conceivably lead to problems later in life.

Often ESL students are extremely shy and never interact with any of their peers. Use the buddy system to address this problem. Whenever you get a new ESL student, immediately buddy him or her up with an English-speaking classmate. The native English speaker acts as a shadow and a helper so you don't have to worry about the new student getting lost on the way to the bathroom or wandering away during recess, etc. Of course, you have to choose your native English speaker "buddy" carefully.

There is a difference between a bilingual and an ESL teacher/classroom. A bilingual teacher is one who speaks the native language of the students and teaches in that native language and in English too. The amount of English depends on the program. An ESL teacher is one who speaks English and teaches the students in English only.

In some parts of the U.S., a bilingual classroom refers to Spanish speaking students and teachers, however in other parts of the country it is common to have bilingual classes for Vietnamese, Chinese, Korean, and many other languages as well. Research shows that it is better to learn in ones native language if possible.

COMMUNICATING WITH THE PARENTS OF ESL STUDENTS

It is as important to communicate with the parents of your ESL students, as it is to communicate with the students themselves. In your weekly newsletter make sure to use lots of clipart for visuals and break the information up into small bites.

Also, provide lots of real visuals at parent orientation and conferences. For example, to demonstrate what the school uniform looks like you could use a stuffed bear dressed in the actual uniform.

To explain that a backpack is required you might hold up an actual backpack. If you have a "no flip-flop" policy, for example, hold up a pair of real flip-flops and shake your head in the no motion and show a thumbs down sign.

Humans are symbol smiths. Written and spoken language are just symbols. While they are highly useful and developed symbols, they are not the only symbols available to use for communication. Remember that and your job will become much easier.

Valentine's Day is a perfect example. This is always a holiday that causes great stress and grief in most ESL classrooms, as it's a holiday that most other countries don't celebrate and the concept of little boxes of school Valentine cards is completely foreign.

You can manage Valentines Day effectively by standing outside the classroom door, a week or two before Valentine's Day and hold up sample boxes of school Valentine cards. You can also copy the front and back of several boxes as examples and send a short note home telling parents where to buy the cards and how to address them. It is a good idea to buy several boxes of school Valentine cards at the after Valentine's Day sales each year because there will likely be a few families who won't comprehend it.

Also, be prepared for students who bring in packages of cards for baby showers, bah mitzvahs, or birthday invitations because their parents just don't understand the concept no matter how hard you tried.

Always be accepting of these situations and never scold the child or demand the parent send in the correct cards. It will only embarrass the parents and student. Just save these cards and put them in your art center the following year rather than send them home and embarrass the family.

ELL (ENGLISH LANGUAGE LEARNER)
IDEAS FOR PROMOTING ORAL LANGUAGE

Word Whacker

Materials: poster board, clipart, glue, scissors, plastic microphone, and fly swatter.

For each theme create a thematic word wall using clip art. Just insert the clip art into a word document and size it to fit your needs, next print it out, cut, and glue the pictures to a poster board. Laminate the poster board for durability. Cut out the middle of the fly swatter with scissors or a knife; the hole will act as a "frame" for the pictures on the word wall.

Next, place the thematic word wall in your large group area and review the words daily with your class. You could do your daily vocabulary review by playing a game called "Word Whacker".

Have a child come to the front and choose either the fly swatter or the plastic microphone. The child gives the other to a friend, whoever has the microphone is the "caller" and whoever has the fly swatter is the "whacker".

The caller calls out a word from the word wall and the whacker has to hit the correct picture with the fly swatter.

Leave this game out during centers and they line up to play it.

Mini-Thematic Word Walls

Materials: cardstock, clip art, laminating machine

Create thematic word walls using the same clip art that you used for the large one. Print the word walls on 8 1/2 x 11 cardstock in your printer, one for each student or table depending on your procedures.

Laminate the mini word walls and place in an area where your students will be able to use them when they write. You will find that these mini word walls really help inspire students to write, by helping to give them confidence.

Pass the Microphone Game

Materials: plastic microphone

This game is super simple and a great oral language developer. Select a question to ask that is related to what you are learning about.

For example you might ask "Do you like cookies?" After you read the story *"If You Give a Mouse a Cookie"*.

Ask the question to a child into the plastic microphone, and the child must answer "Yes, I like cookies" or "No, I don't like cookies"; then he or she asks the question to the person sitting next to him.

Every student gets a turn to ask and answer the question and the person who is very last gets to ask the teacher. They will think this is great fun and always always laugh no matter what your response is.

This game gives students practice in asking and answering questions, using complete sentences, and sentence structure. The later in the year it is the more complex the questions become.

For example, the last week of school you might ask the children "What will you do this summer?"

which requires more knowledge and vocabulary to answer.

You could also play this game after every major vacation, Thanksgiving, Christmas, and Spring Break. It gives them a chance to get back into the routine of speaking English and to share, which all young children love to do.

Color Game

Materials: various colored items, colored poster board 10 clear plastic shoeboxes or cubby bins filled with various items, each box is filled with items of a different color.

Collect the color items from various places, thrift stores, garage sales, fast food toys, and dollar stores.

Each color also has a corresponding poster board shape, red is a circle, green is a square, yellow is a triangle etc.

When you introduce the color box, have all the children sitting in a circle with the poster board shape on the floor in the middle, and then pass the box around the circle and each child takes one item. The child names the item using a complete sentence such as "The shoe is red" and then placing the item on the shape.

This is great for English sentence structure as well as vocabulary because in other languages the noun comes before the adjective (the shoe red) and it takes lots of practice to get them to put the color word first.

After you have introduced a color then put the color box in a center and the students can work with it and play the color game on their own to practice their colors and vocabulary.

It sounds so simple, but it is actually a favorite of most classes. They anticipate each new box and try to guess what might be inside, the first day the box goes into a center they are all fighting over who can play with it first.

Resources for working with English Language Learners

No Limits to Literacy for Pre-K English Learners -Theresa A. Roberts

One Child, Two Languages: A Guide for Early Childhood Educators of Children Learning English as a Second Language - Patton O. Tabors

Many Languages, One Classroom: Teaching Dual and English Language Learners – Karen Nemeth

Easy & Engaging ESL Activities and Mini-Books for Every Classroom: Terrific Teaching Tips, Games, Mini-Books & More to Help New Students from Every Nation Build Basic English Vocabulary and Feel Welcome! - Karna Einhorn

25
Dismissal

Dismissal time is just as important as arrival. If procedures are not in place at the end of the day you can easily lose track of students.

For large schools with crowded dismissal areas it is best for each teacher to have an icon or shape to represent their class as we discussed in Chapter 6.

Create a large "pick-up" card, approximately 4 inches x 9 inches, for each parent with the same icon and the child's name written across the front in large letters. This will help your dismissal time go smoothly and avoid potential problems before they occur. For

186

example, if your symbol is a star, create cards for each parent with the same star and write the child's name across the front in large letters using a permanent marker.

One of the greatest fears any parent has is that their young child will not return home on the first day of school. To start off the school year on the right foot with parents it is important that you make every effort possible to ensure that their child goes home the correct way.

This is the teacher's responsibility because young children don't always know how they go home or they may not be able to communicate it clearly to you. Another concern is custody issues. It is important that young children are picked up by the correct person each day and you, as the teacher, are aware of who they go home with. A sure fire way to end up on the 6 o'clock news is to lose a child on the first day of school.

Most childcare centers have elaborate check-in and out-systems to ensure the safety of each child, public programs often have fewer safeguards so be prepared to create your own using the ideas in this chapter.

For students who ride the bus it's important to group them according to bus number so you don't have to shout out "Who rides bus #45?" which they never know anyway. Instead, line students up by bus numbers and have a distinct way to identify each group.

You can do this by putting a stripe of different colored masking tape at the top of each student's nametag. Place a matching piece of colored masking tape on the floor to indicate where the students who ride each bus should line-up. For example all the red stripes ride bus 45 and are standing on the red line on the floor.

You could also attach a brightly colored shape to represent each bus to the back of student's backpacks or shirts. Attach a matching shape to represent each bus to the wall and have your students line-up next to the matching shapes. Whatever method you choose you must be able to quickly and easily identify each child to ensure they go home on the correct bus.

Closing Thoughts

I hope that you find the ideas shared in this book helpful in your journey as a professional educator. Teaching young children can be exhausting and overwhelming at times, but it can also be very rewarding. One thing I've learned from working with children from around the world is that they are just as eager to learn as you are to teach them. Remember, the best ideas are borrowed. Don't waste time trying to reinvent the wheel, just try to keep it rolling!

ABOUT THE AUTHOR

Vanessa Levin is a passionate advocate for high-quality early childhood education. She has taught in public programs that serve English Language Learners and at-risk populations for two decades. She has served as a teacher, mentor, curriculum writer, specialist, and professional development consultant.

Vanessa is also the creator of the popular website, www.pre-kpages.com where she shares photos, activities, printables and more with early childhood educators around the world.

Vanessa's professional development sessions offered throughout the U.S. and Canada are highly sought after for their emphasis on teacher-tested, hands-on learning activities designed to help all young children meet their full potential in fun, developmentally appropriate ways.

For more information about Vanessa please visit:
http://www.pre-kpages.com/about/

Made in the USA
Middletown, DE
27 November 2017